ONCE UPON A RHYME

IMAGINATION FOR A NEW GENERATION

Southern Counties Vol I
Edited by Sarah Marshall

Young Writers

First published in Great Britain in 2004 by:
Young Writers
Remus House
Coltsfoot Drive
Peterborough
PE2 9JX
Telephone: 01733 890066
Website: www.youngwriters.co.uk

All Rights Reserved

© Copyright Contributors 2004

SB ISBN 1 84460 601 5

Foreword

Young Writers was established in 1991 and has been passionately devoted to the promotion of reading and writing in children and young adults ever since. The quest continues today. Young Writers remains as committed to engendering the fostering of burgeoning poetic and literary talent as ever.

This year's Young Writers competition has proven as vibrant and dynamic as ever and we are delighted to present a showcase of the best poetry from across the UK. Each poem has been carefully selected from a wealth of *Once Upon A Rhyme* entries before ultimately being published in this, our twelfth primary school poetry series.

Once again, we have been supremely impressed by the overall high quality of the entries we have received. The imagination, energy and creativity which has gone into each young writer's entry made choosing the best poems a challenging and often difficult but ultimately hugely rewarding task - the general high standard of the work submitted amply vindicating this opportunity to bring their poetry to a larger appreciative audience.

We sincerely hope you are pleased with our final selection and that you will enjoy *Once Upon A Rhyme Southern Counties Vol I* for many years to come.

Contents

Bethersden Primary School, Bethersden
Chelsea Snow (10)	1
Peter Oliver (11)	1
Tyler Weller (10)	2
Shannon Roles (11)	2
Susanne Buckley (9)	3
Andrew Charlwood (10)	3
Sam Wells (10)	4
Emily Chaplin (10)	4
Megan Slater (9)	5
Naomi Caulfield (11)	5
Abigail Barton (10)	6
Victoria Morgan (11)	6
Matthew Davidson (10)	7

Copthorne School, Crawley
Milan Nayee	7
Tabitha Worsley (8)	8
Poppy Latham (8)	9
Thomas Skiggs	9
James Peek (9)	9
Charlie Ead (9)	10
Ben Swadling	10
Kai Everington (8)	11

Cranleigh Prep School, Cranleigh
Bradley Skillicorn (9)	11
Jasmine Reeve (8)	12
Bea Stephenson (9)	13
Hetty Cunningham (10)	13
Luke Prosser (9)	14
Alexandra Buchanan (10)	14
Henry Thomas (10)	15
Sam Snelling (9)	15
Henry Graham-Rack (9)	16
Bertie Chambers (10)	16
Alasdair Young (10)	16
Hannah Wolstenholme (10)	17

Fergus Brown (10)	17
Charlie Hughes (10)	18
Thomas Lyster (10)	18
Georgia Roulston (10)	19
Dominic Howell (9)	19
Peter Thomas (9)	19
Hannah McLaughlin (10)	20
Lucy Williams (10)	20
Imogen Thomas (9)	21
Alexander Clarke (9)	21
Buchan Richardson (9)	22
Samuel Knight (9)	23
Megan Townsend (9)	23
Gemma Coppe (9)	24
Oscar Reeve (10)	24
Hattie Jones (9)	25

Darell J&I School, Richmond

Alice Weleminsky-Smith (11)	25
Seren Orsman (8)	26
Ozan Yusuf	26
Jake Alder	26
Hermione Burn (8)	27
Joshua Tuckey (9)	27
Flynn Halsall	28
Oliver Bansfair (8)	28
Charlie Kimpton (9)	28
Berenice Cowan (11)	29
Jacob Fisher (9)	29
Farida Khalil	30
Lawrie Colbert (8)	30
Celia Davies (7)	31
Jenny Rogal (8)	31
Ollie Cook (8)	32
Kayleigh O'Brien (8)	32
Daisy Aitken (7)	33
Harry Beechey (9)	33
Rosie Polya (11)	34
Vanessa Zappi-Taylor (9)	34
Christie Eldridge (8)	35
Matthew Pritchard (9)	35

Frank Cook (9)	36
Tom McMichael Armstrong (9)	36
Ambareen Syed (8)	37
Ryan Tyler (7)	37
Amanda Stafford (10)	38
Rebecca Kelleher (9)	38
Albert Brouillard (10)	39
Marsha Aitken (9)	39
Jessica Spahl (8)	40
Elleanore McGlynn (11)	40
Isla Forrester (11)	41
Isabelle Tovey (7) & Rosie Polya (11)	41
Jessica Moos (11)	42
George Reith (11)	42
John Upton (9)	43
Matthew Gilbert (11)	43
Caitlin Jones (8)	44
Anna Mallett (11)	44
Bethan Tingley (7)	45
Jessica Shaw (7)	45
Isabelle Tovey (7)	45
Vanessa Knight (7)	46
Beatrice Zappi-Taylor (6)	46
Findlay Wilson (8)	46
Ben Freeman (7)	47

John Mayne CE Primary School, Biddenden

Abbey Farris (10)	47
Emma Jones (11)	48
Lily-Mae Smith (8)	48
Johnathon Hurcombe (8)	49
Bobby Faulkner (8)	49
Jamie Knott (9)	49
Kelly Archer (11)	50
Sophie Blake (8)	50
Thaliah Dallas (10)	51
Olivia James (8)	51
Adrian Burgess (11)	52
Vincent Gurr (10)	52
Luke Walker (8)	52
Jessica Garrett (10)	53

Kerry Staniland (9)	53
Jessica Penfold (10)	54
Sylvia Penfold (7)	54
Bethany Tester (10)	55
Amy Archer (8)	55
Jack Gracie (11)	56
Amy Brown (10)	57
Lauren Selby (11)	58
Matthew Paul (10)	58
Daisy Tait (11)	59
Lucy Green (10)	59
Laura Hare (11)	60
Bethany Hare (8)	60
Liza Graham (10)	61
William Monk (9)	61
Paul Jones (8)	62
James Paul (8)	62
Carla Roome (7)	63
Polly Morgans (9)	63
Beau Roffey (9)	64
Charlotte Selby (9)	64
Lucy Farris (9)	65
Jack Endersby (8)	65
Conor Prebble (9)	65
Jordan Wilford (7)	66
Danny Weston (8)	66
Richard James Penney (9)	67

Kings Farm School, Gravesend

Kyle Moor (9)	67

Lady Joanna Thornhill Endowed School, Ashford

Suzie Knuckey (10)	68
Grace Scott Deuchar (10)	69

Laleham Lea School, Purley

Ryan Fernandes (10)	69
Jamie D'Costa (10)	70
Marianna Quigley (10)	72

Merlin Primary School, Bromley

Kensey Bryan (10)	72
Rowanne Green (11)	73
Adem Hassan (10)	73
Jean-Luc Wickenden (11)	74
Jack Martin (11)	74
Steven Green (11)	74
Aminu Egenti (11)	75
Katie Walsham (10)	75
Kayleigh Arnold (7)	76
Frankie Simpson (11)	76
Danielle Campion (10)	77
Shivani Modessa (9)	77
James Baker (9)	77
Thomas Blyde (10)	78
Alfie Gill (10)	78
Tegan Maybank (10)	79
Kehinde Akinbode (7)	79
Darcy D'Wan (7)	80
Arlie Desanges (10)	80
Oliver Greene-Taylor (10)	80
Lauren Skinner (9)	81
Denis Blyde (7)	81
Carlos D'Abo (7)	82
Olsi Mataj (7)	82
Hayden Causton (7)	83
Jonathan Faonson (7)	83

Northumberland Heath Primary School, Erith

Leighan Hunt (7)	83
Rebecca Paul (8)	84
Zoe Fortune (11)	85
Leia Elliott (8)	85
Harry Rogers (11)	86
Shaan Sangha (10)	87
Nicholas Hutchinson (11)	88
Hannah Dowsett (11)	89
Hollie Love (8)	90
Joe Davies (11)	91
Latisha Oozageer (10)	92
Sharonpreet Sadhra (9)	93

Hayley Morris (11)	94
Jaspreet Sadhra (8)	95
Richard Masheder (8)	96
Georgina Stock (8)	96
Daniel Page (7)	97
John Boswell (10)	97
Katie Hookway (11)	98
Lilly Webb (8)	98
Julian Bates (10)	99
Sarah Beale (10)	99

Royal Alexandra & Albert School, Reigate

Natasha Gibbons (9)	100
Franny Townsend (8)	100
Chelsea Metcalfe (9)	101
Jack Hart (9)	101
Anji Baba-Ahmed (10)	102
Shannon Chiverton (10)	102
Amy Broad (10)	103
Laura Cogger (10)	103
Shanice Gibbons (9)	104
Ellie Drummey (9)	104
Thomas James (9)	105
Nadia Fowler (9)	105
Elizabeth Kendra (9)	106
Laura Holmes (10)	106
Yasmin Anderson (8)	107
Charlotte Price (9)	108
Vincent Chiu (10)	108
Jack Hawkes (9)	109
Madelaine Hart (9)	109
Amy-Louise Ralph (9)	110
Jessie Sharp (9)	110
Harry Skinner (9)	111
Coralie Glomaud (9)	111
Faye Kennesion (8)	112
Russell Gills (8)	112
Oliver Phillips (8)	113
Raphaelson Aghahan (9)	113
Ana Whittock (10)	114

St Joseph's RC Primary School, Redhill

Jacob McQuillan (10)	114
Florence Pettet (10)	115
Fiona Quinn (10)	115
Zoe-Ann Savage (10)	116
Tobin Jardine (10)	116
Thomas Rowntree (10)	117
Natasha Jardine (10)	118
Jack Dunne (9)	118
Katie Dowds (10)	119
Emma Lewis (9)	119
Isabella Wynn (10)	120
Hannah Jobbins-Hone (10)	120
Jamie Wornham (10)	121
Ruth Connolly (9)	121
Joshua Richards (9)	121
Keelan Twomey (9)	122
Mathew Samuel (9)	123
Sophie Stratfull (9)	123
Rebecca Rogers (10)	124
Kate Stebbings (10)	124
Stephen Murphy (9)	125
Alexander Stearn (10)	126
Alex Ramsden (9)	126
Daniel Sammut (9)	127
Harry Curran (9)	127
Eleanor Heaney (10)	128
Joshua Leigh (10)	128
Helen Redstone (10)	129
Siobhan Robinson (10)	129
Grace Wilson (10)	130
Emily Byrne (10)	130
Hannah Barnes (10)	131
Charlotte Thorne (10)	131
Bella Turner (10)	132
Aaron O'Callaghan (10)	132
Joshua Moore Smith (10)	133
Laura Riddell (10)	133
Devon Bunyan (10)	134
Jessica Leach (9)	134

Thomas Li (10)	135
Olivia Davies (9)	135

St Margaret's At Troy Town CE Primary School, Rochester

Fifi Endrojono-Ellis (9)	135
Liam Dooley (10)	136
Augusta Cook-Overy (11)	137
Rosemary Acton (10)	138
Olivia McGregor & Chantal Isaac (10)	139
Jack Cavanagh (10)	140
Benjamin Brothwell (10)	140
Jake Gurney (9) & Jack Yerrall (10)	141
Jack Paulley (11)	141
Emma Diprose (10)	142
Tommy Boakes (10)	142
Rori Dudley (11)	143
Zachary Lovell (11)	143
Shu Cheung (11)	144
Ben Williams (11)	144
Joshua Hancock (10)	145
Amber Whiting (11)	145
Vabyanti Endrojono-Ellis (10)	146

St Peter's CE Primary School. Folkestone

Joshua Howell	146
Adam Bartlett (10)	147
Beth Gillan (10)	147
Shane Ridley (10)	147
Sebastian Weightman (10)	148
Kayleigh Gilson (10)	148
Ellen Gregory (10)	148
Jaryd Lohan (11)	149
Robbie Westbrook (10)	149
Chani Sanger (10)	150
Zoe Chapman (9)	150
Michael Bridges (11)	151
Naomi Nicol (9)	151
Zoe Perry (10)	151
Natalie Atherton (11)	152
Marcus Williams (11)	152
Bradley Weightman (11)	152

Daisy-May Weightman (9)	153
Shunna Wallace (9)	153
Jordan Redworth (9)	153
Jaye Mynard (11)	154
Jake Gregson (10)	154
Caroline Wiechmann (7)	154
Gabriella Dawkes (11)	155
Elliot Langston (10)	155
Marcus Palmer (11)	155
Albert Gregson (9)	156
Simon Gillan (8)	156
Leigh Chapman (8)	156
Damon Greenway (8)	156

Sedley's CE Primary School, Southfleet

Ellie Hardinges & Louis Milioto (7)	157
Philippa Coppitters (8)	157
George Summerfield (9)	158
Annabel Coppitters (9)	158
Ellie-Rose Thomas (7) & Chelsie Fuller (8)	158
Hannah Mitchell (8)	159

Sellindge County Primary School, Ashford

Daisy Cropper (10) & Alex Hyder (11)	159
Ryan Martin (10)	160
Matthew Pryce (7)	160
Demi Williams (11)	161
Emily Hare (9)	161
Liam Bishopp (9)	162
Rionne Tucker	162
Billy Cross	163
Joseph Beaney (8)	163
Ronny Shorter (11)	164
James Ashman	164
Jack Stephens (11)	165
Bryony Homewood	165
Chelsea Williams	166
Jed Deal	166
Shannon Houghton (11)	167
Amber Bull (7)	167
Lauren Burgess (11)	168

Lewis Coates (9)	168
Emel Larsen (8)	169
Megan Bishop	169
Ashleigh Williamson (11)	170
Shelby Kennett	170
Abdul Ahad (10)	171
Kerrie Alexander (9)	171
Shanon King	172
Lauren Hyder (8)	172
Sharon Fuller (9)	173
Kerrie Alexander (9)	173
Nishat Rashid (10) & Suzanne Curtis (11)	174
Bethany Old (7)	174
Joshua Walton (10)	175
Joe Williams	175
Roanna Williams (11)	176
Yasmin Shorter (8)	176
Liam Bailey (11)	177
George Tanner (11)	178
Katherine Pryce (10)	179
Alexander Yardy (10)	180
Sam Baker (11)	180
Harry Stephens (8)	181

Shernold School, Maidstone

Liberty Francis (10)	181
Jamie Thresher (8)	182
Rhea Tanna (9)	182
Methula Nanthakumasan (10)	183
Bethany Gerrish (10)	183
Ben Harvey (9)	184
Nancy Watts (10)	184
Alexandra Browne (11)	185
Christabel Webb (9)	185
Hamish Massie (7)	186
Tom Cosgrove (9)	186
Alice Jepheart (8)	186
George Edwardes (11)	187
Edward Craddock (10)	187
Ami-Kay Gordon (8)	188
Anna Davis (9)	188

Pranav Kasetti (9)	189
Shelby-Jo Bellamy (10)	189
Joanna Harvey (7)	190
Charlotte May (10)	190
Michaela Savage (11)	191
Abbie Prentice (8)	191
Lourdes Webb (11)	192
Foluso Shoneyin (10)	192
Elizabeth Blenkinsop (8)	193
Jordan Tompsett (8)	193
Lauren Lethbridge (8)	194
Chloe Funnell (8)	194
Megan Leach (9)	195
Thomas Scoley (7)	195
Chanel Levy (9)	196
Eleanor Pile (8)	196
Emily Witney (9)	197
Niroshan Ravishankar (9)	197

Temple Ewell CE Primary School, Dover

Emily Martin (8)	198
Kenny Jones (9)	198
Elizabeth Williams (9)	199
Ashley Mills (8)	200
Holly Gillard (8)	200
Caroline Padfield (9)	201
Lauren Beaney (8)	201
Elliot Cox (8)	202
Finlay McMunn (8)	202
Paris Bates (9)	203
Olivia Kurzawa (8)	203
Drew End (8)	203
Georgia Berry (7)	204
Amber Harrison (8)	204
Katerina Vause (7)	204
Kayleigh Steele (7)	204
Charlotte Ward (9)	205
Hollie Pain (8)	205
Rachel Grant (9)	206
Jason Mallory (8)	206
Callum Moorin (9)	207

Ashley Tse (8)	207
Matthew Bryant (8)	208
Katie Williams (9)	208
Dominic Hayles (9)	209
Carla Reid (8)	209
Chloe Thomson (9)	210
Luke Hind (9)	210
Becky Matthews (8)	211
George Smissen (9)	211
Jessica Dowle (9)	212
Cerys Wilmshurst (8)	212
James Phillips (8)	213

Upton Primary School, Bexleyheath

Sadie Smurthwaite (10)	213
Emily Giles (8)	214
Colina Archie-Pearce (9)	214
Lucy Robinson (9)	215
Zara Nosratpour (9)	215

The Poems

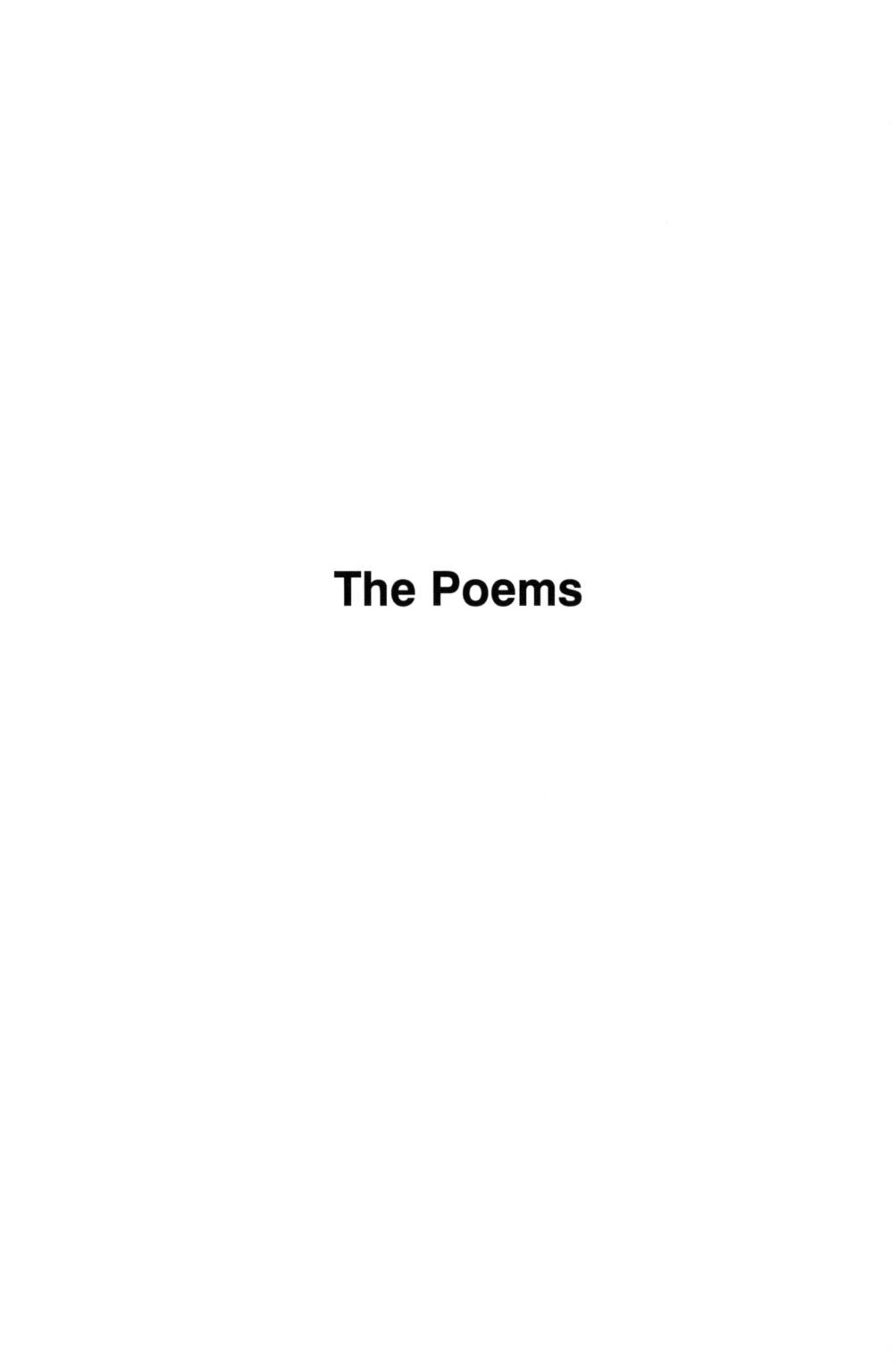

Animals

There was a strange pig,
It was wearing an enormous wig.

I saw a mysterious cat,
It was wearing the most extraordinary hat.

There was a peculiar cow
It said, 'Look at me! Wow! Wow! Wow!'

I saw a funny little dog
It was sitting on a very disgruntled hog.

There was a sad old sheep
It was very sad, it was being sold very cheap.

I saw a magnificent horse
It galloped round and round and round.

All these animals are great
I wish they were my mate!

Chelsea Snow (10)
Bethersden Primary School, Bethersden

Mr Marvolo

Mr Marvolo was short and thin
Was almost as short as a drawing pin.
He went to the doctor's on Thursday
And the doctor said, 'You're going to fade away.'
Mr Marvolo went home very sad
But even he felt a little mad.
He took one blink and a tear fell down
When his eye opened he started to peer
He started to peer at a short thin lady.

He walked up to her and said, 'Hello.'
And she replied 'Hello to you.'
They both went home holding hands
And he still had that tear in his eye.

Peter Oliver (11)
Bethersden Primary School, Bethersden

What Am I?

I'm slippery and I'm slimy
And I go crunch
I am also a bird's lunch,
I don't have wings and I don't have a tail
Yes, you've got it I'm a snail.

I live in a tree
But you can't live with me
I hope you heard
Can you guess? I'm a bird.

I like to hop
And I never stop
I don't go fizz and I don't go pop
I like everyone and I like you
Yes, I am a kangaroo!

Tyler Weller (10)
Bethersden Primary School, Bethersden

Lion Cub

The day my lion had a cub
I gave my cub a little rub.

The cub wanted its mum,
And I said, 'Go have some fun.'

The cub came running up to me,
And took my funny key.

My cub and Mum followed me,
To play with me in the big blue sea.

They splashed me,
In the sea.

We ran back home,
And played in the Millennium Dome.

Shannon Roles (11)
Bethersden Primary School, Bethersden

My Pets!

I have four pets
Berlious, Cupcake, Honey and Nets.
Berlious is a cat,
Nets is a rat,
Cupcake is a horse
And Honey is a hamster of course.
Berlious is black and white
So you can't see him at night.
Cupcake is a dapple-grey
And she loves lots of grass and hay.
Honey is ginger
And she acts rather like a ninja.
Nets is brown,
And he always has a frown.
They're all good friends
But this is the end
Of my poem.

Susanne Buckley (9)
Bethersden Primary School, Bethersden

The Rushing River

The raging river is always flowing,
Never knowing where it's going.
Where it will always be crashing,
And unexpectingly bashing.
When it's gnawing on the pebbles of the beach,
Crashing bashing out of reach.
When it sweeps round the bends,
But never, ever ends.
The river always has a magical flow,
Why? No one knows.

Andrew Charlwood (10)
Bethersden Primary School, Bethersden

Family Pets

All the pets that I have got,
Yes I have a lot.
A dog, a rabbit, I got them all,
Even seven horses they're very tall.
Birds and hamsters I love to cuddle tight,
All through the day and sometimes in the night.
I love my pets so much,
All of them have a furry touch.
But mostly I love Treacle Bear
She is my hamster, I love to take care.
I want to ride the pony I've got,
If only he wasn't a soppy pot.
So these are the pets I have with love,
And if they pass on, I hope they go above!

Sam Wells (10)
Bethersden Primary School, Bethersden

The African Sunset!

Just as the day is dawning,
The sun wakes up stretching and yawning.
Then above beams a moonbeam sky,
As the sun rises high.
Shining over the African sea,
All the animals skip with glee.
But soon enough the day goes past,
As the sun starts setting fast.
Camels lay down on the sand,
The big ball of lava blazes across the land.
Blazing across like a thundering fire,
Shining by the palms it's the animals' desire.
Then it leaves a trail of red,
And disappears down the horizon to go to bed.

Emily Chaplin (10)
Bethersden Primary School, Bethersden

Sleeping Beauty

Sleeping Beauty just nodded off!
On the bed so nice and soft
All the kingdom is wondering
Who will wake her and be king?
A great forest grew all around
Thorns and thistles filled the ground!
Until one day a prince came by,
When all the thorns were up to the sky!
He gallantly cut them down
Upon his face he wore a frown
When he found her he kissed her on the cheek!
Then Beauty woke up to speak
Beauty said, 'I love you'
And the Prince said, 'I love you too!'

Megan Slater (9)
Bethersden Primary School, Bethersden

The Big Red Blob

The big red blob was in my shoe,
Out the window it flew, flew, flew.
The big red blob was odd, odd, odd,
It was born in a little red pea pod.
The blob followed me, sneaking behind my back,
All the way home, on the train track.
I shouted, *'Go away!'*
But he wanted me to play
He started to sob,
The big red blob.
At last it ran away,
I told it I didn't want to play.

Naomi Caulfield (11)
Bethersden Primary School, Bethersden

My World

Anything I think of goes into my mind,
Leaving the normal world behind.
I sometimes think of places I'd like to go to, like Spain
But then I remember boxing where people feel pain.
Ice cream, sweets, chocolate and more,
More sweets than the ones that made you sore.
A yellow sun on a summer's day
With a swim in the sea as you may.
Skipping to the park with a friend or two,
Or maybe it just might be you
Climbing a tree bold and tall,
Not like a plant tiny and small
Prince and Princess dance till nigh,
Sailing away up so high into the sky.
A pirate or two fighting till death,
Taking their last breath.
As I fall asleep in my bed,
I think that's all that needs to be said.

Abigail Barton (10)
Bethersden Primary School, Bethersden

Sabrina

A girl named Sabrina who lived in a quiet neighbourhood
was a young witch but some of her spells didn't do any good.
She lived with her aunts and an old black cat
Sabrina is not a witch who has a wand or black hat.
Her friend Harvey does not know she is a witch and she has a talking
black cat, or she has a magic flying mat
but when she was invited to the witches' ball,
Salem said, 'One of your spells will make you stand from them all!'
And so she did, she went to the ball,
And danced with young wizards, all very tall.
Sabrina was a happy girl, a very happy witch as well.

Victoria Morgan (11)
Bethersden Primary School, Bethersden

Jack And The Beanstalk

Jack was a poor, poor lad
Daisy the cow was all he had
but he swapped her for some beans
and thought about them in is dreams.

The next morning he awoke
up the tree he saw a bloke
he was very tall and big
in his arm was a golden pig.

Jack took it to his mum
this stopped her from being glum
he climbed back up the very tall tree
to see what he could see, see, see.

Then he stole a golden hen
and then went up the tree again
he went back up for the third time
this time the giant saw his crime.

The huge great giant was very fast
but then Jack escaped at last
with an axe he chopped the tree down
the giant came tumbling with a great big frown
they lived happily from that day on
all because Jack had some wrong.

Matthew Davidson (10)
Bethersden Primary School, Bethersden

Haiku

Autumn is the best
as the leaves come falling down
in colourful shapes.

Milan Nayee
Copthorne School, Crawley

Funny Fish

I like funny fish
Because they do tremendous tricks
Like making doughnuts dance
And bounce big, big balls.

Funny fish pounce
On the river bank
They also like to make jolly jokes
And eat the water worms.

They eat big burgers
And get fat fast
They always swim stupidly
And have evil looking eyes.

They splish and splash
Because they find it lots of fun
The noises make the crabs so annoyed
They clip and clap their pincers at all of them.

They always go to fancy fairs
And always brush their funny fur
They also melt magnificently
And always halt heavily.

They all should be in the fish circus
To say their jolly jokes
And do their amazing acrobats
But best of all twinkle their tails.

Splish, splosh, splash
Their tails go when they swim
They only do this because they are proud of themselves
And they like to annoy the fattest of the crabs.

Tabitha Worsley (8)
Copthorne School, Crawley

Poppies

Pretty poppies open their petals in spring.
Pansies appear to be poppies' best pals.
Farm fields are full of flowers.

People walking past often pick poppies,
Then pansies want to be picked as well,
So they can prance one more time.

Then poppies go to sleep for a while
And then wake up again.

Poppy Latham (8)
Copthorne School, Crawley

My Visit To The Zoo

The big blue bus took us to the zoo
The angry, agitated apes let me through the gates
Karate kangaroo kicked the cow when it moved
Minging monkeys munched on mushy mangoes
The lazy lions laid in their lair laughing at the hapless hare
A super snake slithered through the slimy grass
The terrifying tiger did a tremendous roar
The big baboon's bulging bottom was as red as a slapped cheek.

Thomas Skiggs
Copthorne School, Crawley

Ducks - A Haiku

A dewy morning
Ducks sculling in crystal ponds
Hiding in water.

James Peek (9)
Copthorne School, Crawley

The Sun

Sun shines stunningly
On the green grass
Gleaming golden
As an angel
The sun shines stunningly
Fiery fun
I am amazed
Boy, it's a boiling sun!
Fun, fun, fun!
Whirling wind
Oh no!
Hurry in the house!
Oh the rain, rotten rain
Oh look, the stunning sun
Over outside again.

Charlie Ead (9)
Copthorne School, Crawley

The Fête

The fantastic fun-filled fête
Fish and fancy clowns
Food, fun and don't be late.

Clowns, circus and coconuts too
Carriages, cakes and chocolates
All the fun without the zoo.

Bouncies, booths and hundreds of balls
Burgers, bands and bottles
Fun's over, I'm trapped again inside
The walls.

Ben Swadling
Copthorne School, Crawley

My Bedtime Haiku

I snore in the night
In my comfy, little bed
While round me lies night.

Kai Everington (8)
Copthorne School, Crawley

Christmas Dog!

In
the
house
at
Christmas
time,
our dog
plays with
the Christmas
pine
up he goes
with a bauble
on his nose,
oh! he's having
so much fun,
playing with
his Christmas
bun. He's always
getting
wrapped in
tinsel.
That is how
he got his
name.

Bradley Skillicorn (9)
Cranleigh Prep School, Cranleigh

The Land Of Boggeldy

In the land of Boggeldy Boo,
There was an elephant wearing a shoe,
The shoe was pink with bright green spots
She had three babies in three cots.

In the land of Boggeldy Bee,
There were two fish and one was me,
I was orange, my friend was green
There was another who acted mean.

In the land of Boggeldy Bum,
There was a tree that grew a plum,
The plum was orange but somehow turned green
But nobody knew where it had been.

In the land of Boggeldy Bong
There was a church with bells that went 'dong'
The church was brown and very tall
There was a skeleton in the hall.

In the land of Boggeldy Boil,
There was a garden with lots of soil,
The garden was pretty with one big rose,
But later that evening it fell on my toes.

In the land of Boggeldy Bop
There was a town with one big shop,
The shop sold peanuts and lots of toys,
And in it there were lots of boys.

In the land of Boggeldy Bap
There was a track and I ran a lap
I was not very fast,
So of course I came last.

So if you live in a Boggeldy land
Then you may only have one hand,
But if you've seen one of these strange things
Then you will probably have secret wings.

Jasmine Reeve (8)
Cranleigh Prep School, Cranleigh

Cows

There once was a baby cow
With a green spot
Who went to bed in a cot.

His brother was clever
And had a blue stripe
He went to bed in a pipe.

His mum was a cleaner
Who had a purple mop
And went to bed with a sock.

His dad was a chef,
Who had a very fat tummy,
And he went to bed with a dummy.

Bea Stephenson (9)
Cranleigh Prep School, Cranleigh

War!

Cries of a wounded man
Seeing people die
Shells exploding everywhere
Coldness, sadness you have to bear
Hunger, worry about your friends
If you live it depends
You have to obey all the commands
Otherwise you'll be shot
In the night it's dark and scary
And when you wake up it's war again.

Hetty Cunningham (10)
Cranleigh Prep School, Cranleigh

My Grandma

My grandma is the best
She helps the bluetits with their nest.

She runs around playing with me
Then we go inside for tea.

My grandma loves her flowers
She gets really happy when there's April showers.

My grandma is really funny
She says she's met the Easter bunny!

My grandma's sailed on loads of ships
Then she comes back for fish and chips.

My grandma's eyes are as blue as the sea
I love it when it's just Grandma and me.

But most of all she's loving and kind
Such a good Grandma's hard to find
And I love her the best!

Luke Prosser (9)
Cranleigh Prep School, Cranleigh

War

Cries of a wounded man
Seeing people die
Shells exploding
The sound of machine guns banging,
My eyes watering from the gas,
Staring out at no-man's-land,
The yells of people above
People shouting at me
It is so scary,
I hate the war.

Alexandra Buchanan (10)
Cranleigh Prep School, Cranleigh

War

The deafening cry
of a wounded man
The awful sight of
dead bodies lying
around on the streets.
Suicide bombers killing
little innocent children
like you or me.
Guns spitting out death,
threatening bullets killing
innocent civilians.

Henry Thomas (10)
Cranleigh Prep School, Cranleigh

Just Dreaming

School's boring
I'm snoring
I'm sleepy
You're creepy.

>I nod off
>You drop off
>Mr Gainher
>Tells us off.

>>I said,
>>'I'm just
>>Dreaming.'

Sam Snelling (9)
Cranleigh Prep School, Cranleigh

The Mace

One day in space
I was having a race.

Suddenly a mace hit
Somewhere on my face.

I fell out my ship, did
a double backflip.

The ship came down
then hit the ground.

Henry Graham-Rack (9)
Cranleigh Prep School, Cranleigh

War

People dying everywhere
Machine guns firing heavy bullets
Canons firing shells
Exploding all around.

Air raid sirens screaming
Dive bombers shooting from the air
People of the war dying
Cries of men becoming silent.

Bertie Chambers (10)
Cranleigh Prep School, Cranleigh

War

Sobbing for a wounded man
Quick, run back if you can!
Shells exploding all around
Men falling to the ground
A chatter of a gun over there
All I could do was stare!

Alasdair Young (10)
Cranleigh Prep School, Cranleigh

Mrs Gravill

She's a warm comfy sofa
She's a soft bed
She's a cuddly kitten
She's a lovely rabbit
She's a lovely sandy beach
She's a beautiful flower garden
She's a nice choir singing
She's a violin making a lovely sound
She's a shining morning
She's a glimmering morning
She's a sun
She's a star.

Hannah Wolstenholme (10)
Cranleigh Prep School, Cranleigh

War

A whistle blew in my ears
Do you know what this meant?
We had to go over the top
So off we went.

And then I heard it - a machine gun rattle
Taking down men in this tremendous battle.
I saw a shell soaring down
Bang!
I hit the ground without a sound.

Fergus Brown (10)
Cranleigh Prep School, Cranleigh

Bertie!

He is a wobbling cushion
He is a hard table
He is a springy chipmunk
He is a furry hamster
He is a mossy living room
He is a mad moth
He is a roaring lion
He is a squeaking violin
He is a mad bath in the evening
He is a crazy lunch
He is a speedy torpedo
And a whirly hurricane.

Charlie Hughes (10)
Cranleigh Prep School, Cranleigh

The Day I Will Never Forget

The cries of a wounded man,
The day I will never forget
All the shells exploding in a horrific trench.

Seeing all those people die,
I felt sick and wanted to lie -
On the muddy, wet ground
Death is written on every face
Death is written on every soldier's soul.

Thomas Lyster (10)
Cranleigh Prep School, Cranleigh

War

Shells exploding in a trench
The fight out to no-man's-land
Planes crossing in the air
Bang, bang, bang
There it goes again
Snow falling from the sky
Tiredness growing, growing
In the darkness I can hear singing
And then smack, my head hits the ground.

Georgia Roulston (10)
Cranleigh Prep School, Cranleigh

Rugby Ball

There is a man who's very tall
And look he's got the rugby ball!
The crowd is roaring mad,
They're shouting *'He's the lad!'*
Look he's on a fantastic run
Golly he must be having fun
He's jumped very high up into the sky
Now he's falling down . . . and it is a *try!*

Dominic Howell (9)
Cranleigh Prep School, Cranleigh

The Cricket Match

'C atch that he must be out!'
  R oared the crowd with a shout
   I am desperate to win this match
  C ould I take a catch?
   K ings come from all around
    E veryone makes some sound
     T he kids are playing in the stands.

Peter Thomas (9)
Cranleigh Prep School, Cranleigh

Mum

She's a bouncy bed
She's a big cuddly bear
She's a jumping kangaroo
She's a fast cheetah
She's hot Australia
She's cold England
She's a roaring lion
She's a quiet mouse
She is the afternoon and
                    the night
She's a beautiful princess
She's my cuddly mummy.

Hannah McLaughlin (10)
Cranleigh Prep School, Cranleigh

War!

Cries of a wounded man
Seeing people die,
Seeing people dead,
She's exploding so near
Machine guns killing
Thinking you're going to die
Hearing people shouting,
Hearing people screaming,
Trenches killing your soul!

Lucy Williams (10)
Cranleigh Prep School, Cranleigh

Strange Animals

In a field there was a foal
The strange thing was it lived in a hole
It became very fat
The sad thing is, it loved a pat.

In a lake there was a frog
The strange thing was, it lived on a log
Its favourite food was purple flies,
His best thing was to tell big lies.

There once was a little mouse,
The strange thing was he had his one house,
He had a tiny little mouse mat,
On which he keeps his favourite hat.

There once was a parrot called Polly
Who was the colour of Holly
Her best friend was Monkey Mop,
The funny thing was he had to hop!

Imogen Thomas (9)
Cranleigh Prep School, Cranleigh

My Brother's Birthday

It's my brother's birthday,
And my friends won't help!
My brother walks towards me,
And I start to yelp!
Each step by step he gets closer,
Looking at me with glee!
He extends his short arms and . . .
Oh! He's got a present for me!

Alexander Clarke (9)
Cranleigh Prep School, Cranleigh

Rugby

Robinson on
the ball,
He is taking it into
a mall,
He dropped it into rum,
Now it is a
Scrum!

    Wilkinson
    does a fling,
    All the way out to
    the wing,
    Cohen is covered in muck,
    From the bottom
    of the ruck.

England
have won
From a try by the run
Italy have lost
Driving in a load
of compost.

    Let's have a
    look at the replay,
    Just to finish the
    day.
    That's the end of the
    game,
    And Italy are in shame.

Buchan Richardson (9)
Cranleigh Prep School, Cranleigh

My Brother

My brother thinks he's the king
And wears a twenty-four carat gold ring!

My brother thinks he's a popstar,
So he shouted 'I am a rockstar!'

My brother thinks he's a chicken,
Oh how his head seems to thicken!

My brother thinks he's Robby Keane,
But really he plays like Mr Bean!

My brother thinks he's Martin Tyler,
But really he's a big skiver!

My brother thinks he's made of lead
Uh-oh it's time for bed!

Samuel Knight (9)
Cranleigh Prep School, Cranleigh

My Friend

She is a bright light always on
She is a bouncy trampoline
She is a new dog wanting a walk
She is a strong kind rabbit
She is a busy little bee
She is a singing robin
She is a famous popstar
She is a sunny morning with a bright blue sky
She is a bright star.

Megan Townsend (9)
Cranleigh Prep School, Cranleigh

A Crazy Classroom

My classroom is mad,
You have to have a pad,
Because if you don't
You really won't
Be feeling very glad.

My class is cool,
We have a pool,
We have a swing, stupid thing,
We have some games,
With silly names.

Gemma Coppe (9)
Cranleigh Prep School, Cranleigh

War

Shells are falling all around
The crack of rifle sounds
The man now falls onto the ground.

I see men running
Bang, bang, whack,
Brits are shouting, 'Look at that!'

It's my turn now to go over the top
A shell just landed next to me
It blew my leg off, can't you see?

Oscar Reeve (10)
Cranleigh Prep School, Cranleigh

War

The banging and clanging of shells,
the people crying,
children screaming for their mothers,
then suddenly you hear the screech of the air raid siren,
the planes flying overhead
then all you hear is the distant ringing of the siren.

Far . . . far . . . far . . . away . . .

Hattie Jones (9)
Cranleigh Prep School, Cranleigh

Breath Of Life

Rippling waves, a graceful sea
A wandering horse willing you closer
His gleaming white coat and startling eyes
Making you wonder how he glides

The glittering waves sucking you in
A whistling wind making your eyes water
The tide lapping against your feet
Life and death soon shall meet

The gleaming horses suddenly smirk
This was a trick made to fool
Made for those who love the waves
Hope falling like sun's rays

But no one can trick those who love
Only those who hate can be tricked by God
Water cannot cut like a knife
Can only give the breath of life.

Alice Weleminsky-Smith (11)
Darell J&I School, Richmond

Weather Talk

'Smashing weather,' said the forecast
'Smashing weather today, there'll be
sunny spells around the east.'

Does it mean glass will smash as it falls?
I don't know.
Will the sun cast a spell on us?
I hope not.

'Howling wind we will have today
I hope you will not get blown away.'

Will a wolf howl on a mountain?
I hope so too because I don't want to
be blown away.

Seren Orsman (8)
Darell J&I School, Richmond

The Summer Wind

The spring wind is calm and warm
The autumn is greedy and a mystery.
The winter wind is rough and tough
The summer wind is nice and white.
The summer wind, the amazing things it can do
Cleaning the world with its humongous wings.

Ozan Yusuf
Darell J&I School, Richmond

The Summer Wind

The spring wind is clear and fresh
The autum wind is vicious and colourful
The winter wind is strong and cold

The wind I love the best.

Jake Alder
Darell J&I School, Richmond

Weather Talk

'Raining cats and dogs,' said the forecaster
'It will be raining cats and dogs today.'

Does that mean there'll be
wild dogs chasing after everyone?
Or does it mean the poor cats
will be running for dear life?

Or maybe even the poodles will jump
out of the clouds?
Do the tabby cats get special wings to
fly down to Earth?
Or does it mean you can
get a pet for free?

That would be too cool for me.

Hermione Burn (8)
Darell J&I School, Richmond

The Winter Wind

The summer wind
is nice and bright
The spring wind
is warm and free
The autumn wind
is colourful and rushing.

The wind I love the best
is strong and mean
quick and nasty
and mad and wild
but that is the wind for me.

Joshua Tuckey (9)
Darell J&I School, Richmond

The Autumn Wind

The autumn wind
is vicious and wanting.
The spring wind is calm and bright.
The winter wind
is strong and it might give you a fright.

The wind I love the best
comes after spring,
and when it comes the wind goes calm,
sweet and smooth.
So summer is good for me.

Flynn Halsall
Darell J&I School, Richmond

The Winter Wind

The summer wind
Is soft like cotton
Autumn wind I've nearly forgotten
Spring wind
Is like a snake.

But my favourite is winter break
Winter wind is like a solid cake
It's also like someone's hate.

Oliver Bansfair (8)
Darell J&I School, Richmond

The Summer Wind

The spring wind is calm and gentle
The winter wind is rough and misty
The autumn wind is vicious and colourful.

The wind I like best is kind and warm
It is the summer wind that blows my troubles away.

Charlie Kimpton (9)
Darell J&I School, Richmond

Sea Of Words

The sea
A serene blue stone upon our Earth
Yes, that is the sea
But not my sea
For my sea is a sea of words.

The sea
Islands of swirling ink-filled pages
These wonders are my sea
Not wet, but dry
An ocean of memories, ideas, delights.

Fantasy forever flowing
Whispering
A sea, an ocean
A book.

Berenice Cowan (11)
Darell J&I School, Richmond

The Winter Wind

The summer wind
is calm and gentle
The spring wind
is clear and free
The autumn wind
is rushing and swirling.

The wind I love the best
brings ice and mist
The winter wind
brings snow, bringing fun for everyone.

Jacob Fisher (9)
Darell J&I School, Richmond

The Summer Wind

The summer wind is hot and warm,
It's calm and good for lots of things,
I'm sure the breeze on the farm,
Is gentle and warm and calm.

The summer wind is sometimes cool,
And by now caterpillars turn into cocoons
The swallows would really like this weather,
And in the swimming pool children will play together.

When it comes to night-time in summer,
The wind is cool and cold weather,
Sometimes in summer, it starts to rain,
And what bad weather it is to train.

Farida Khalil
Darell J&I School, Richmond

Weather Talk

'Raining cats and dogs,' the forecaster said.
'It's raining cats and dogs today.'

But how can it be raining cats and dogs?
Did God invent a new type of poodle
that can fly or can live for ever?

And cats will have eighteen lives instead of nine
or could the badly treated cats and dogs
want revenge?

And I'd like to know what is in a weatherman's
pockets of rain,
not very good sunshine that's for sure.

Lawrie Colbert (8)
Darell J&I School, Richmond

Secrets Of The Sea

Rock pools filled with sloshy water
Red jelly-like sea anemones
Slowly waving sticky tentacles
Small green crab
Scuttling in and out of its hole

Wavy, rough sea
Special orange fish with black tail
Sliding and gliding by a rock
Yellow and silvery fish
Swimming in shoals.

Spiky black sea urchins
Watch out! They might poke you.

Celia Davies (7)
Darell J&I School, Richmond

Weather Talk

'Smashing weather,' the forecaster said
'Smashing weather today!'

So does that mean the sun will turn into a giant
and smash up the town?
Or will the rain start to turn into glass
and smash into tiny bits when it hits the ground?

Or like last week, the forecaster said
'Sunny spells today'
Does that mean the sun is going to turn us
into frogs or pigs or dogs?

Jenny Rogal (8)
Darell J&I School, Richmond

Weather Talk

'Uncontrollable winds,' said the forecaster
'There'll be uncontrollable winds today.'
So does that mean
Someone controls the winds
Using a remote control like a toy aeroplane?

'It's raining cats and dogs,' said the forecaster
Does that mean
There'll be poodles in our tube stations?
Cats landing in our driveways?
And kittens in our local library?

'Boiling-hot today,' said the forecaster
Does that mean you'll be boiled alive?
Steam everywhere and you're in pain?
Do you get burnt on the spot
Because giants think you're the egg they dropped?

The weather forecaster is nuts.

Ollie Cook (8)
Darell J&I School, Richmond

The Winter Wind

The winter wind
is misty and strong
The autumn wind
is colourful and wild
The spring wind
is fresh and warm.

The summer wind
is smooth and gentle
and it's calm and soft.

Kayleigh O'Brien (8)
Darell J&I School, Richmond

Brighton Pier

We went to Brighton Pier
Hurrah, hurrah, hurrah
It was very cold
Brrr, brrr, brrr
We went on the dodgems
Bump, bump, bump
Mama hurt her neck
Ow, ow, ow.

Dada won a hulkie
Wow, wow, wow
We didn't win a monkey
Boo, hoo, hoo
We rode on the baby dodgems
Hee, hee, hee
Martha went on the dance mat
Stamp, stamp, stamp.

I went on the ski boat
Ski, ski, ski
We bought some rock
Yum, yum, yum
Then we went home
Bye, bye, bye.

Daisy Aitken (7)
Darell J&I School, Richmond

Weather Talk

'Red-hot,' the forecaster said, 'it will be red-hot today.'
Does that mean the sun will turn red?
Does that mean all the lights go red?
Will the rain be red-hot and will our glasses melt?
Will people with blue eyes have red eyes?
And I'd like to know what's in the weather?

Harry Beechey (9)
Darell J&I School, Richmond

Soul Of The Sea

The seagulls scream, the seals shriek
Foaming waves rise and fall, troubled
Water cries, writhes and dies upon the rock
Icy rain throws itself into the sea
Thunder rumbles angrily
Lightning strikes viciously
Sand drowns under the salty sea.

With a roar so terrible, so sad
A huge creature, scared and frightened
Despite its size, despite its ferocity
Lets out another noise
Even more sad and heartbroken
Feeling emotions so deep and sorrowful
That no one else could ever feel them

Then the creature dived, into the world below the air
Below the sea, below our world and into despair
The sea calmed down, the sun came out
The rain stopped
And all was like it was before the creature came
But all the animals that had witnessed it
Were never the same
The creature had broken their hearts too.

Rosie Polya (11)
Darell J&I School, Richmond

Weather Talk

'Red-hot sun,' the forecaster said
'There'll be red-hot sun today.'

So does that mean that you'll be boiled alive?
Will you be baked while walking across the road?
Will your house get so hot that you will be killed?

Vanessa Zappi-Taylor (9)
Darell J&I School, Richmond

When I Look Into The Sea

When I look into the deep blue sea
I see a reflection
A reflection of me.

I see lots of fish all coloured bright
As they swim side by side
They shimmer in the light.

The waves crash upon the sand
They hit the rocks
With the sound of a marching band.

Children are swimming, having fun
While mums and dads
Lie in the sun.

Surfers are surfing in the sea
Splashing people
Especially me.

Christie Eldridge (8)
Darell J&I School, Richmond

Weather Talk

'Rainy spell,' the forecaster said
'There will be a rainy spell today.'
So does that mean the rain will turn us
into something?

'Heavy rain,' the forecaster said
'There will be heavy rain today.'
Does that mean the rain will hail us
to the ground?

Matthew Pritchard (9)
Darell J&I School, Richmond

The Changing Sea

The sea is never the same
Once rushing, once lame
Once it was a bed of nothing
Then it was suddenly slushing
Once I went to see the sea
Slapping, crashing against my knees
Never the same after that
As it washed away my hat
Out to sea my hat sailed

It was thunder crashing, lightning flashing
Boat tipping, side smashing
Man crashing, heart pounding
It was bad, it was loud
Dangerous, bottomless
Crunching, rough,
Don't go to the sea with your hat.

Frank Cook (9)
Darell J&I School, Richmond

Weather Talk

'Smashing weather today,' the forecaster said
'Smashing weather it will be.'

I wonder what it means?
Does it mean that the glass will fall down on my head?
Smashing weather it will be.

I wonder what's next?
Smashing weather today
I think they are lying
Smashing weather today.

Tom McMichael Armstrong (9)
Darell J&I School, Richmond

Whole Of Blue

See the water rippling across
The smooth and bumpy rocks
The sea is getting ready to toss
Then suddenly the water slides
Into your warm socks.

Under the sea's blanket
Lying across the Atlantic
Beneath the shimmering pool
Is the mermaids' swimming school
Which is always bustling with laughter - no rules

The waves silently tumble as the sun drifts
The gentle sunset lifts
Colours of red, orange and yellow
The colours of a musical cello.

The crest of dancing waves
Somersault sharp and soft
Washing onto gritty sand
That's the fascinating whole of blue.

Ambareen Syed (8)
Darell J&I School, Richmond

Chiswick House

One fat cat,
Two tall towers,
Three big bricks,
Four tall trees,
Five red roses,
Six tall tables,
Seven fat frogs.

Ryan Tyler (7)
Darell J&I School, Richmond

Seashore Show

From our Earth on land, still is the ocean
But underneath there is a commotion
While tuners play tunes on the tuna
And eels play octaves on the octopus
By playing scales they are flattened
In order to keep the rhythm going.
Starfish act like they are stars
And clownfish make jokes to amuse the crowd.

Crabs click their claws to keep the fish dancing
And the leaders of the dancing are two Spanish lobsters
Using their claws as castanets while doing Spanish dances.
Pufferfish blow into their trumpets
To help keep the rhythm going
And a school of young whales sing in harmony.

What dancing, what singing, what a band
All underneath the sea on the sand
And that is what keeps the sea's rhythm going.

Amanda Stafford (10)
Darell J&I School, Richmond

The Sea

Yesterday it was as stormy as a hurricane
As loud as a thousand trumpets
As rough as a tough giant
It moved like an angry monster
Thumping its fists.

Today it's as still as a statue
As quiet as a mouse
As smooth as silk
It moves like a baby
Walking its first steps.

Rebecca Kelleher (9)
Darell J&I School, Richmond

The Fisherman

There once was a fisherman who had a tiny boat
He only went fishing in a storm.

Then one day our teacher said, 'Work Experience'
So I went with the fisherman.

His name was Ted
We went out in the storm.

It was so rough
But he was tough enough
To fight the storm.

I'm writing this from an unknown island
I don't know where he is.

Albert Brouillard (10)
Darell J&I School, Richmond

The Sea Is A Changeable Thing

The sea is a changeable thing

Like a lion opening its huge jaws
And tasting the salty air.

Like a puppy waiting for you
To throw a stick over the smooth sand.

Like a fire burning the tips of your toes
Whispering its spell.

Like a giant snoring
Chest heaving up and down.

The sea is a changeable thing.

Marsha Aitken (9)
Darell J&I School, Richmond

Weather Talk

'It's raining cats and dogs,'
The forecaster said,
'Just raining cats and dogs.'

So does that mean kittens and puppies
Are going to fall down
And land in my back garden
And walk into the kitchen
Looking for food?

Or does that mean that cats and dogs
Will crash through your umbrella?

Well I think the forecaster
Doesn't have kittens in his pocket
That's for sure.

Jessica Spahl (8)
Darell J&I School, Richmond

My Fish

I see my fish in the calm gentle water
I see my fish amongst the ponds
Where there are trickling sounds
I see my fish within the gentle tides
I see my fish amongst the soft prancing waves
I see my fish flow along with the waves.

The waves are crashing now
The waves are tumbling
The waves are high and loud
The waves are bellowing.

And I can't see my fish.

Elleanore McGlynn (11)
Darell J&I School, Richmond

The Sea Dragon

The sea dragon looks monstrous, is monstrous
But to me he is calm, he is gentle
He swishes about in the violent sea
He brings death to anyone who comes near him
Except me, he knows me.

He is friends with the white horses
Who run night and day
They know me too
The sun is setting
It's red, a red-hot sun shining down.

The sea laps and fights against the cliff
Shattering the rock that sinks to the sea bed
Falling on top of the sea dragon
I calm him because I know him
For I am a mermaid.

Isla Forrester (11)
Darell J&I School, Richmond

Ten Things Found In A Mermaid's Pocket

A rainbow coloured hairbrush
Magic mirror
Pearl jewellery box
The biggest and most beautiful shell on Earth
A princess' crown
A key to the secret castle under the sea
The tastiest sweet ever
The yummiest cake ever
The sweetest smelling flower in the world
A golden cup that lets you live forever.

Isabelle Tovey (7) & Rosie Polya (11)
Darell J&I School, Richmond

The Mourning Sea Horses' Song

Many mortals walk the sands of the sea
Writing poems about swishing waves and white gulls
                                          screaming
But mere morals do not hear
The whinnies of the sea horses' song.

They sing of times with great elves hither
Their horses kept all wild and free
Yet after the age of fantasy thither
The mortal man turned all to stone.

The snorts of the great sea horses
Carry on through time and all
They sing the song of freedom
And stories of great elven halls

And mortals stroll along the beach
Deaf to all they sing
Though all would not believe the tales
Of the great elven king.

Jessica Moos (11)
Darell J&I School, Richmond

The Widow

The sea seemed empty all until
Her face appeared without will
Bearing no longer her love
Flooding the ocean with her tears
Her cry no longer heard above.

And sat in front of her last friend
She sang to him upon her lips
A song unheard by mortal ear
And as she withered she showed no fear
Except that of an immortal tear.

George Reith (11)
Darell J&I School, Richmond

The Sea

Sometimes I am calm
But sometimes I am angry
Pushing and pulling a foamy wave
That's how I behave

I can contain great pain
Or great joy . . . or both
I can contain a battle
Or a man

I contain life
Swimming in me
I can make it angry
Or wash it away like rolling a finger over a desk.

I can also kill
Anything within me
Break a boat
That's how strong I am.

John Upton (9)
Darell J&I School, Richmond

Drifting

Drifting along on the sea
Randomly floating, moving up and down in the breeze
I would love to be free
Forever drifting in the sea.

To be here forever more
In a place of peace
Not a single law
Getting away from the seashore.

Matthew Gilbert (11)
Darell J&I School, Richmond

At The Sea

At the sea, today
The sun is heating up the sand
The pebbles are lying silent and still
The boats are having their quiet talk
While the children are jumping to the bottom of the sea.

Rock pools are splashed by the children and their nets
Pelicans and seagulls are flying round and round
Making a cute little noise
A grunt and a squeal
And other boats are bobbing up and down.

Ice creams are melting
From the hot sunny sky
Now it's time to be going
So we'll all say goodbye.

Caitlin Jones (8)
Darell J&I School, Richmond

Soldier

Soldier
Holds his breath
And cocks the pistol
Breathes deeply
Takes careful aim
Biting his lip
Pulls back the trigger
Wondering if he's now a murderer.

A few months later
He sits at home
And kisses his daughter goodnight.

Anna Mallett (11)
Darell J&I School, Richmond

Playtime

I am very lonely
I don't like it
Nobody is nice to me
They all play with their friends
But me, I don't have any friends
I stay in the corner of the playground
This happens every day.

Bethan Tingley (7)
Darell J&I School, Richmond

Finland

I want to jump about
I want to dance
I am happy all over
I can hear music in my brain
I feel like I am swinging on a trapeze
My heart is beating with joy
I am going on holiday to Finland.

Jessica Shaw (7)
Darell J&I School, Richmond

My Dad

My dad comes back from holiday
I am very happy to see him
And he is very happy to see me
He gives me a cuddle
I get a warm feeling all over
We love each other very much.

Isabelle Tovey (7)
Darell J&I School, Richmond

The Sea

The sea is bottomless and blue
Deeper than me or you
About as deep as 1084 shoes
Perhaps deeper
Who knows?
Not me
But who?

Vanessa Knight (7)
Darell J&I School, Richmond

In The Middle Of The Night

It is dark
The floor is creaking
The wind is whistling
Everybody is sleeping
Except me.

Beatrice Zappi-Taylor (6)
Darell J&I School, Richmond

Waves

Smashing waves
Making caves
Rocks bashing
Ships crashing
That's how the sea behaves.

Findlay Wilson (8)
Darell J&I School, Richmond

I Am Confused

My brain is weak
My brain has switched off
My brain is quiet
My brain is in a world of its own
I don't feel like me
I don't know what's up there
Right up in my head
But I know that it's something *bad!*

Ben Freeman (7)
Darell J&I School, Richmond

A Day Out

Got up early, went on a run
A beautiful day in the sun.
Laura tripped over a little stone
She had a bad cut and you could see her bone.

We made our way to the dining hall,
The breakfast wasn't ever cool.
Later we went on a hike
It would have been easier on a bike!

We came up to a massive hill
Walking back up it really kills
Making wishes, walking through trees
Countryside that's all we could see.

I climbed up high
On a forty-foot tower
Daisy's name
Was Flower Power.

Speeding round orange cones
Flicking up little stones.

Abbey Farris (10)
John Mayne CE Primary School, Biddenden

Zip Wire

I walked slowly to the bench,
Feeling nervous.
What if the rope snapped?
What if I fell off the tower?

It was finally my go,
Gingerly I climbed the stairs
He called me up and clipped me on.

Time to drop
I dived off the top
My heart was pounding
As I hung in the harness.

I dropped the rope
And Ken pulled me down
I was safe
On the ground!

Emma Jones (11)
John Mayne CE Primary School, Biddenden

In Space

A stronauts fly around
S un hits the planets all day
T he hot galaxies move once a day
R ockets, spaceships fly in the air
O rbit in space
N o oxygen comes! Help!
A ll nine planets move round the sun
U nknown planet has been found in space
T he space flows by in silence.

Lily-Mae Smith (8)
John Mayne CE Primary School, Biddenden

What Is Sun?

What is sun?
Sun spot, sun flares, dark red patches, sun . . . very hot,
dead sun, sun gas.

What is sun?
A yellow star, radioactive sun, hot gasses.

What is sun?
The red star, light, 4.7 billion years old.

Johnathon Hurcombe (8)
John Mayne CE Primary School, Biddenden

What Is Yellow?

What is yellow?
A yellow car that is shiny
Yellow chalk, yellow shapes and yellow books

What is yellow?
The sand is yellow, flowers and yellow boxes.

What is yellow?
Yellow umbrellas, trees and scissors.

Bobby Faulkner (8)
John Mayne CE Primary School, Biddenden

Waterfall

A wonderful sight of gushing water
A crashing hazard
Rushing to the waterfall relentless wrecking
Going down the waterfall.

Bursting waterfall
With a rapid flow
Crackling like bubble wrap
Water blasting down the vertical drop.

Jamie Knott (9)
John Mayne CE Primary School, Biddenden

Challenge Course

Following the lady,
She was called Kate.
Wearing our muddy pigtails
To meet our fate.

We stood inn a line,
Looking at the mud
It was disgusting
Then I heard a thud.

It was Abbey,
Making a splash
In a massive puddle
We made one big bash.

A short time later
We got hosed down
Abbey was the muddiest
She should have worn a crown!

Kelly Archer (11)
John Mayne CE Primary School, Biddenden

The Colour Yellow

The hot sun,
The sun is very hot,
It is very blazing hot.

Yellow daffodils,
Yellow banana,
Yellow book

Gold diamond crown
Gold necklace
Gold clothes and shoes.

Sophie Blake (8)
John Mayne CE Primary School, Biddenden

Waterfall

Flowing, surging down
Through the cracked cliffs
Tumbling, spitting bubbles
Nothing left alone.

The river is moving fast
Where is it going?
It's coming straight down,
You better be aware!
Waterfall!

Now its found its way into
The deep dark mouth
Closer and closer it gets to the delta
Cracked rocks can't stop it
Now it's gone too far, how
Many seconds till it gets to the . . . sea.

Thaliah Dallas (10)
John Mayne CE Primary School, Biddenden

Yellow Paint

Yellow paint drips falling to the ground
Making big
Yellow puddles
Flowing everywhere.
Under gates
Through drains
Under doors
Going everywhere.

Olivia James (8)
John Mayne CE Primary School, Biddenden

Tornado

Energetic, fast tornado comes across the land
He's got a plan!
Sucks a can up, lands on somebody's head.
Guess what he did? He pleaded.

Now it's time to destroy!
Pick up houses, like a toy.
Then drop them on the ground
What a noise.

Spinning rapidly out of control
Disappears deep into a hole.

Adrian Burgess (11)
John Mayne CE Primary School, Biddenden

The Deep Water

Crashing bashing
Into the river
Soon the stones will go
Tumbling and turning
Into the deep water.

Vincent Gurr (10)
John Mayne CE Primary School, Biddenden

Space Poem

P eople explore space
L ovely enormous plants
A liens everywhere in space
N ASA rockets flying in space
E ngines are roaring in the rockets
T urning round to land
S paceship is landing, zooming fast.

Luke Walker (8)
John Mayne CE Primary School, Biddenden

The Waterfall Journey

I was born at the mountain top
Running faster down
Gushing unable to stop
Twirling round and round

Crashing bashing through the rocks
Gravity is pulling me down
As bouncing off the rocks violently
Making a lot of sound

I was once a towering boulder
Now a pebble really small
Ending this part of my journey
At the deafening waterfall.

Jessica Garrett (10)
John Mayne CE Primary School, Biddenden

The Waterfall

Rapid river,
Gushing, twirling around
Splashing crystals are shining
Lost as soon as they are found.

Crashing, tumbling,
A tall lady in a cloud-white gown,
Bursting silk and delicate lace,
Is rushing down.

Deep, spooky, roaring,
She now starts to shiver,
Faster, faster down the river,
It has reached the river!

Kerry Staniland (9)
John Mayne CE Primary School, Biddenden

The Deep Ravine

The river enters the deep ravine,
It suddenly goes quiet.
The only noise is the drips falling into the water from the
moss above your head.

As you yell, *'Hello!'*
All there is is the echo of your voice
The moisture in the air makes you cold and shiver.

Suddenly the river urges to go faster,
Faster and faster as it zooms through the deep ravine until
It gets to the . . . d
                                       r
                                       o
                                       p
                                       !

Jessica Penfold (10)
John Mayne CE Primary School, Biddenden

Spacesuit

S tars so beautiful in the sky
P eople fly in the dark sky
A naughty alien disappears
C reepy noises go to your ears
E ek! Let's get out of here
S ome planets rock and roll
U gly aliens go out at night
I think it's time to get a fright
T onight I'm getting out of space.

Sylvia Penfold (7)
John Mayne CE Primary School, Biddenden

The Waterfall

I am a giant granite boulder
Perched precariously on the mountain top
Now tumbling and turning
Into the deep choppy waters I drop

Water bursting and bubbling
Aqua-blue and snowy white
Pushing and shoving
Being pushed along by the river's might

I'm crashing and bashing
Getting chipped in the flow
Want to go fast
But don't want to go slow.

As I come to the sea
My outside is smooth and sleek
I am a pebble now and into the sea I sneak.

Bethany Tester (10)
John Mayne CE Primary School, Biddenden

My Space Poem

S tars are twinkling
P lanets are floating
A stronauts are flying
C reepy aliens are eating
E ven you can see Earth
S pace shuttles are zooming
U gly aliens are everywhere
I 'm scared of them
T onight I'm coming home.

Amy Archer (8)
John Mayne CE Primary School, Biddenden

The Wall

Walking through the wood,
With my mate
Hands feeling sweaty
Fast heart rate.

The wall stood in front of me
Ever so high
Would I get the chance
To say goodbye?

We stood in the line
Oh so tall
Put me in a harness
So I wouldn't fall.

The instructor yelled out, 'Jack
It's your go.
Fast as you can.'
I'm going slow.

I'm climbing the wall now,
Muscles really hurt.
If I'm not careful
I'll end up in the dirt.

Finally I've done it
I've reached the top
They lower me down
To avoid the drop.

I feel really proud
And oh so cool
Somehow I've managed
To defeat the wall!

Jack Gracie (11)
John Mayne CE Primary School, Biddenden

Waterfall

I am a massive boulder
At the very top of a mountain
Rushing down
Splashing
An elegant fountain
As pointed as a crown

Now I am getting nearer
Scraping past the rock
Dreading the crash
Closer, closer
Nearing the drop
I fear the thought in my stony head.

I am being pushed out
Over the edge
    Bash
        Crash
            Bursting
                And bubbling
                    Tumbling and turning
                        To the bottom of the
                              W
                              a
                              t
                              e
                              r
                              f
                              a
                              l
                              l

Amy Brown (10)
John Mayne CE Primary School, Biddenden

Volcano

I stand still under the ground
Then a bubbly noise is found.
I get a temperature, burning hot,
I'm very calm, I think not!

I'm loud and destructive, people beware
Please watch out and take great care.
I get in a temper, spitting out gunk,
People thought I really stunk.

I've done my duties
I'm ready for bed
It's time to rest
My sleepy head.

Lauren Selby (11)
John Mayne CE Primary School, Biddenden

The Waterfall

Huge white figure touching the sky
Dark blue water tumbling off its head,
It cascades down the huge statue
Like her flowing to the ground.

Sun shining warmly
Stroking the zooming water
As it tumbles down the cliff
Like an aeroplane whizzing towards the
Ground.

The noise of the falling water
Keeps you alert,
Banging and crashing
Water falling like it will never end.

Matthew Paul (10)
John Mayne CE Primary School, Biddenden

My Adventure Week

On the first night
We couldn't get to sleep
We wouldn't see our parents
For a whole week.

We did some cool activities
During the next day
It was wicked and amazing
What more can I say?

Everyone thought
The food was rough
Everyone agreed
The mud challenge was tough!

I flung down the zip wire
At an amazing speed
When Abbey reached the top
She screamed her need.

On the quad bikes
I went on two wheels
Lauren laughed her head off
Boy, did she squeal.

At last it was
Time to go home
How nice it would be
To sleep alone.

Daisy Tait (11)
John Mayne CE Primary School, Biddenden

The River

The water is bashing its way down
As the gravity is pulling
As the river goes faster the river can't stop
And soon it goes to the . . .
                                    . . . drop!

Lucy Green (10)
John Mayne CE Primary School, Biddenden

Challenge Course

The challenge course awaits us
We've no idea what's ahead
Ready to get muddy
We start to roll in water.

Caked in mud
From head to toe
We scrambled in the muck
To try and reach the end.

Kate said we were too clean
So she made us put our heads in puddles
Now we're dripping wet
With twigs and leaves in our hair.

But everything comes to an end
We walked away
Our clothes drenched
We were a sight for sore eyes.

Laura Hare (11)
John Mayne CE Primary School, Biddenden

Spacesuit

S hooting stars flying past
P lanets you have never seen before
A liens creeping up behind you
C ounting stars . . . there are millions!
E ven you can see the amazing Mars
S paceships shoot past
U ntil I reach home I'm alone
I 'm waiting patiently
T onight I am proudly coming home.

Bethany Hare (8)
John Mayne CE Primary School, Biddenden

The Ravine

You tiptoe in
Shivering cold and bare
Wind rushes right
Through you
You're not alone.

You cautiously sneak
Into the ravine
Further and further
Damp and slimy.

It rushes closer and
Closer, through the dark galley
It zooms
Rushes
Scrambles
Until . . .
Suddenly . . .
Drop!

Liza Graham (10)
John Mayne CE Primary School, Biddenden

What Is Yellow?

What is yellow?
The hot fiery, a yellow basket, juicy bananas and yellow pineapples.

What is yellow?
Yellow stickers, yellow book, some yellow plants like a very big planet Saturn.

What is yellow?
Yellow shoes, yellow stones, yellow light.
Yellow planet, yellow football, yellow leaves and yellow paint.

William Monk (9)
John Mayne CE Primary School, Biddenden

What Is Yellow?

What is yellow?
The big hot sun
And lovely bananas,
Big and juicy.

What is yellow?
The lovely sandy beach
And big pretty sunflowers
And lovely buttercups.

What is yellow?
A pair of yellow socks
And a big yellow dress
And a yellow planet.

Paul Jones (8)
John Mayne CE Primary School, Biddenden

What Is Yellow?

What is yellow?

The blazing hot sun, bright yellow buttercups, daffodils and delicious, bendy bananas.

What is yellow?

A pair of different colour socks, dark yellow paint and soft sandy beaches.

What is yellow?

A big alien, squidgy butter, a dog, a colouring pencil and the colour of a mask.

James Paul (8)
John Mayne CE Primary School, Biddenden

My Space Poem

S un is red, orange and hot gas
H uge big planets
O ne planet is called Jupiter
O ne of the planets is called Saturn
T hey test the rocket
I nside the enormous space shuttle
N oisy alien
G lowing alien

S tars are blue, red, white and yellow
T est the blast off
A stronauts are hard to move
R ockets have a bang when they go up
S aturn is the second big planet.

Carla Roome (7)
John Mayne CE Primary School, Biddenden

My Space Poem

In space . . .
Red spaceships, blue and green
The most amazing thing you've ever seen
Mars Jupiter and the great big sun
Come up here, it's really fun.
Wow! Look there's the moon,
We will be coming back soon.
Aliens are big and hairy,
You mustn't forget they're very scary!
Then the rocket took off with a whoosh and a roar,
And came whizzing down to Earth's floor.

Polly Morgans (9)
John Mayne CE Primary School, Biddenden

My Space Poem

S hooting star
P lanets circle around
A stronauts in space
C ircle round planets
E ager aliens coming to invade

S paceship gas into space
H eight is the worst thing
U niverse is enormous
T he big solar system
T onight I am going home
L anding at the space station
E ven we are not in space.

Beau Roffey (9)
John Mayne CE Primary School, Biddenden

What Is Yellow?

Yellow is the runny yolk of an egg, yellow is the hot
burning sun, yellow is steaming hot fire.

      What is yellow?

Yellow is ripe, lovely, delicious bananas ready to eat,
yellow is cold orange juice, yellow is the bright stars
that shine, yellow is the rough sand.

      What is yellow?

Yellow is Saturn with brown lines of stone,
yellow is ripe, juicy, sweet peaches with banana ice cream.

Charlotte Selby (9)
John Mayne CE Primary School, Biddenden

What Is Gold?

Shining gold coins waiting to go in the till
Six gold crowns getting stolen
Golden lions roaring in the distance
A massive gold fire burning hot
Gold paint waiting to be used
A golden chain people wear
A golden egg geese lay.

Lucy Farris (9)
John Mayne CE Primary School, Biddenden

What Is Gold?

What is gold?

The gold crown and pencil,
Gold space rocket,
Gold trophy, gold football,
Gold certificate.
Gold watch, gold water bottle
That is gold!

Jack Endersby (8)
John Mayne CE Primary School, Biddenden

My Space Poem

P eople explore enormous space in spaceships
L ovely peaceful place to be
A liens on planets all day
N ight-time all the time in space
E arth to space from space station
T ime to go back to brilliant Earth
S paceships land really fast.

Conor Prebble (9)
John Mayne CE Primary School, Biddenden

My Space Poem

S hooting stars are yellow and white
H ot sun is red and orange
O rbiting planets
O ut around the sun
T ime's running out
I n the space shuttle all is ready
N o one must be left behind
G oing to the solar system

S paceships are white and big
T hey go into the black space
A nd see the shooting star
R ight in the sky.

Jordan Wilford (7)
John Mayne CE Primary School, Biddenden

What Is Yellow?

What is yellow?
A yellow lemon cake with lemon icing
A pair of stinky yellow socks
And buttercup which flowers a lot.

What is yellow?
A great big sandpit that shines of yellow
And a yellow sunflower.

What is yellow?
A bright yellow football
And the sun that shines every day.

Danny Weston (8)
John Mayne CE Primary School, Biddenden

The River

Crashing, bashing
Into the banks
Tumbling, turning
Bursting and bubbling
Water splashing
And flowing.

Jumping, cracking open
The stones
Flooding over the banks
And rushing to the sea.

Richard James Penney (9)
John Mayne CE Primary School, Biddenden

Kite

Dancing in the air
Breezes push left and right
A ghostly being
In the sky
String
s
t
e
a
d
y
l
i
n
g.

Kyle Moor (9)
Kings Farm School, Gravesend

Pixies

Silently, cautiously, the little pixies step
Round the corner on the rug where Crimson Whiskers slept.
Climbing up and down from the fridge
As silently as a midge
Then down they go
To a gentle whistle that they blow.

Underneath the floorboards there,
Pixies are feasting on jelly and pear.
Shouting little pixie words,
Sounding like little chirping birds,
Pixie children prancing around
A matchstick they have found.

But up above the uproar
Crimson Whiskers is waiting for?
Waiting for, when the time is right,
When the male pixies take flight
To gather more food for all,
He will pounce, gobble them up, one and all.

Very soon that time came,
But the pixies saw the flame.
His tail go swish,
They knew his wish,
Pixies crept silently away,
Not near danger would they stray.

Then creeping back to their hole
With the food they stole,
Thank goodness they had packed much food
To content their winter mood.
Very soon Crimson Whiskers will get tired
And in his dreams he will be admired.

Suzie Knuckey (10)
Lady Joanna Thornhill Endowed School, Ashford

Mourning

She lay on her bed, drenched in death
Her skin was marred by a yellowish mark
Her poison stained lips were silent and blue
As she lay in the haunting dark.

Her sea of coal hair was tangled and matted
Her violet eyes were unblinking and wide
I was blind to the fact, as I stood by her bed
'Twas three weeks ago, sweet Lily had died.

Her pure white skin was as soft as ever
Yet her muscles were never again to be used
Her body was like a dressmaker's doll
And her pale face was cruelly bruised.

Never again did I enter that room
Lily was left lying dead
Never again did I enter that room
Where tears for my Lily were shed.

Grace Scott Deuchar (10)
Lady Joanna Thornhill Endowed School, Ashford

At The Seaside

Down by the sea
A creature said to me,
Come and see
The little lea.

I held the water with my hands
And looked abroad for golden sands,
But first, I saw a secret garden
Filled with fruits and blooming flowers
I stared at it for hours.

Many pleasant places more than
I have ever seen before
The meandering river passed me by
With ships and boats docked nearby.

Ryan Fernandes (10)
Laleham Lea School, Purley

Kenning

Got a sense of humour
When he is angry he is a fumer,
Not sporty,
Quite naughty.

Young professor,
Teacher stresser,
Evil scientist
Bendy contortionist.

Guitar strummer,
To him school is a bummer,
Music lover,
Big Bruvver.

He is ten,
Got a blue pen,
Loves jelly,
Watches the telly.

Likes D12
Arsenal smell,
Hockey is cool,
But chess rules.

Marvellous whizz-kid
Balancing on top of a dustbin lid,
Drinks coke,
Likes telling jokes.

Story writer,
Never a biter,
Supports Liverpool
He is not a fool.

Busted hater,
Do your homework! Later
Young rockstar,
In chess he'll go far.

Untidy locker,
Justin Hawkins is a rocker,
He plays the drums,
While doing hard sums.

I am a boy,
Got an Xbox for a toy,
Many animals he owns,
My fat dog has bones.

Quite clever,
Horrible! Never?
In a band,
I lie in the sand.

Young poet,
All around know it,
I often play ball,
I am quite tall.

Rubbish at art,
Hates raspberry tart,
Dandy dresser,
Mum stresser.

Now at last my poem is nearly done,
I hope you had a lot of fun,
So have you found out who I am,
I'll give you one more clue so you won't say 'Damn.'

I play rugby,
At two I was in a buggy,
I am quite sly,
I wish I can fly.

If you can't work it out,
You are as silly as a scout,
My name rhymes with Amy,
So come on and name me.

Jamie D'Costa (10)
Laleham Lea School, Purley

Kenning

Chocolate lover
Hates butter,
Don't want to eat a leech,
Adores the smell of bleach
Hates spiders and American ciders.

Loves money to spend
Doesn't always go with the trend
I would like a cake and a milkshake,
I have long hair
And I wouldn't say I was contrary.

January is my birthday,
That's far away,
I'm good at netball,
I often fall.

Girls rule, boys drool,
Girls are thin, boys are dim
That's what I say,
If you can't guess it today
Then carry on anyway,
It's easy-peasy who it is.

Marianna Quigley (10)
Laleham Lea School, Purley

Lonely Spider

Hairy and rough
Stuck in a web
Crawling around
Doesn't know
Where to go
Lonely, sad,
All alone by itself.

Kensey Bryan (10)
Merlin Primary School, Bromley

Calm Waters

The top of the ocean so calm and still,
Yet no one knows the secrets that lie beneath.

The still, slow tide devours the cliff face,
The twinkle of the ocean's eye,
Spies on up above.

The sea creatures are all around,
The chatter of the dolphins
Like the creak of a door.

It's nearly the end,
The sun is setting,
And soon an ocean will appear above me.

Until . . .

The top of the ocean so calm and still,
Yet no one knows the secrets that lie beneath.

Rowanne Green (11)
Merlin Primary School, Bromley

Rubbish Old Trainers

I started off new and shiny.
They really loved me and
they always washed me.
One day I got a bit dirty
and after I was worn out
they never washed me ever again,
so now I'm as nasty and dirty as a messy pig.
I never have feet in me now and
I feel really sad and lonely.
The children have new trainers
and I used to be the best, but I'm not now.

Adem Hassan (10)
Merlin Primary School, Bromley

The Bird Of Flight

It flies as quiet as a butterfly,
Its claws are like sharpened blades,
The feathers are like a fur coat that I would buy,
And it is as big as a bus
It's do or bust.

It is as white as snow
Its feathers have a silky glow,
I would steal you but oh no, no, no, no,
Close your eyes let it whoosh past, it's like an open window.

Jean-Luc Wickenden (11)
Merlin Primary School, Bromley

The Love Poem

You are so fine,
Would you be mine?
You could share some wine,
Would you be mine?
You are a shine,
Would you be mine?
You are so fine,
So would you be mine?

Jack Martin (11)
Merlin Primary School, Bromley

Night

Night is a time to sleep and think of the things that matter,
How I hate the night when the bogeyman comes to eat me.
I saw him in my room so I went under my covers
And called my mum to say, 'I ain't having fun,'
So I put on my scary mask and scared the bogeyman away
For another day.

Steven Green (11)
Merlin Primary School, Bromley

The Phoenix

It burns down from the Heavens
In a fiery flame
Its wings are like burning blades.

It swoops down like a fireball
Hurtling towards the Earth.

Its feathers are a new brand
Its claws are fiery daggers
And across it staggers.

It's nothing like James Henry Trotter
It's like the Fire bolt out of Harry Potter.

And now it shrinks as small as a dove,
Giving out all its love.

There and then on the hill it dies
Leaving, for us, lovely apple pies.

Aminu Egenti (11)
Merlin Primary School, Bromley

Mouldy Spider

Slowly he tiptoed into the corner
with his pointy feet leaving spots
on the ceiling.

Looking down sharply
with his bright red eyes,
there was . . .
a creepy looking spider.

He had mouldy grey spots
over his black spiky skin
with his white bright fangs catching
the light.

Katie Walsham (10)
Merlin Primary School, Bromley

Night-Time

All the stars are shining bright
You can see the beautiful moon
Even though the sky is dark
There are lots of beautiful lights everywhere.

This is when you close your eyes
You dream about your wonderful future
Listen to your lovely lullaby
Stay with your dreams until morning.

Now is when you rest in bed
Forget about all your stress
Think about the brightest star
Rest your head upon your pillow.

The stars form a constellation
Don't wake up for hours
Let your bad times leave you
The time has come for sleep.

Kayleigh Arnold (7)
Merlin Primary School, Bromley

Summer

Summer is coming prepare for fun
Light is coming, that means sun
Lots more children come out to play
Because we will have a lot more day.

The ice cream man will make a lot more money
Because it will be hot and sunny
At the end of another summery day
Winter will be on its way.

Frankie Simpson (11)
Merlin Primary School, Bromley

Summer Blossom

I slowly float from side to side
falling from the tree
And when I land
I lay quiet and still
on the wavy flowing grass
and sometimes
I even cover the floor
with my light pink petals like a carpet.

Danielle Campion (10)
Merlin Primary School, Bromley

Spiky Spider

Crawled in the corner
Looking bristly and spooky
His hair is prickly like a hedgehog's back
He was a lonely fellow
That lived in a corner of a house
But with no tiny gaps.

Shivani Modessa (9)
Merlin Primary School, Bromley

Wolves

W ind carrying howls
O n the mountain tops
L iving different country
V ery vicious when seeing prey
E vil eyes of terror
S harp fangs and claws.

James Baker (9)
Merlin Primary School, Bromley

Fierce Dog

They have a rough coat
like a brush.

They have big, bold and
chipped teeth.

Their ears are
red radars.

Their eyes are
big, bright beams.

They have bits hanging from
their claws.

Their smell is fantastic because
they smell things miles away.

Thomas Blyde (10)
Merlin Primary School, Bromley

Tick Tock

Tick-tock, tick-tock
Watch the world go by
looking at my precious numbers.

Tick-tock, tick-tock
Watch everyone pass by
even though I'm not popular.

Tick-tock, tick-tock
With my big hand touching and my little
hand reaching for numbers.
But the thing that bewilders me is
how they get there.
I don't even know how old I am with all
these tick-tocks going on.

Alfie Gill (10)
Merlin Primary School, Bromley

Sunflower's Growing

I start off as a tiny seed
in the arms of the comforting soil.
I need dripping wet water
and the oven of the sunlight.
Then my bright green stem starts to emerge
I'm blinded by the blaze of the sun.
The soil is much smaller and further away
than usual and beneath me,
and after a couple of days
with the blaze of the sun
and dripping wet water
my face will appear
bright brown with yellow hair
sticking out.

Tegan Maybank (10)
Merlin Primary School, Bromley

Playtime

Playtime, playtime, is for a break
you run out and you run in and all the different things.

Playtime is having great fun
you can play Mum's, Dads or ponies.

Playtime is pretending you are big or tiny or
imagining you're huge like a giant that stomps and stomps.

Playtime is great, playtime is wonderful
just have great fun because playtime is brilliant.

Playtime, playtime, you can scream about
because playtime is having such lots of fun.

Kehinde Akinbode (7)
Merlin Primary School, Bromley

School

School is fun, you come to school to learn
All the time you're there you seem to learn something new.
You do all kinds of things like painting, writing, drawing
and reading.
You have to learn to work in groups to get your work all done.
By the time the day is ended, you feel exhausted but want to
stay and learn that bit more.
But now it is time for me to go, because it's time for assembly
Which is one thing you cannot miss.

Darcy D'Wan (7)
Merlin Primary School, Bromley

The FA Cup Triumph

As a swarm of bees they fly
round and round they flow by
as the supporters follow by
oh Millwall oh Millwall
we love you, carry on and
we'll cherish you.

Arlie Desanges (10)
Merlin Primary School, Bromley

A Sofa's Life

The fly lays on its black leather arms
tickling them whilst it looks around the room.

As it sits to attention and the baby dives into
the gaps and creases.

It sits in front of the window
with the gleaming sun shining down
through the window and lays watching the
snow-white clouds of the Earth go by.

Oliver Greene-Taylor (10)
Merlin Primary School, Bromley

A Clock's Story

I'm a friend to everybody
they always stare at me day by day.
I tick-tock to the children as they
come galloping in.

I'm nailed to the wall
but never mind, I'm a useful thing
so it doesn't matter to me.

As the children come in
I get a day older, no one wants to look
at me, no more.
So I guess I'll stop working.

They try to change my batteries
but I go slower and slower
and my hands no longer sweep
past my face.

I'm tossed out into the bin
the dustbin man never seems to notice me
as my beauty fades away
I try to push my hands away from my face
but I don't have no energy.

I should just wait until the next load come crashing
in, and maybe I could meet some friends
and sit on the pile of litter, chattering away.

Lauren Skinner (9)
Merlin Primary School, Bromley

School

I go to school and I'm angry
I go to school and I'm fed up
I go to school I'm tired
I go to school and I like learning
I go to school and like doing PE.

Denis Blyde (7)
Merlin Primary School, Bromley

Night

In the dark of the night I fall over
I bump my head on the floor
My mum puts me on her bed
because I won't bump my head on the floor.

It's too hot
sometimes when it's hot I stay up late
on the internet with my sister.

On Sunday I go to bed really early
because Monday is school day.

When it's cold I go straight to bed
because I feel tired.

When it's school day I go to bed early
because I love school, I don't like to
be late for school.

Sometimes I play questions with my mum.

Carlos D'Abo (7)
Merlin Primary School, Bromley

Night

At night I never get any sleep
because I get a weird dream,
when I sleep only I stop it.

At night I get hot but I take my trousers off
but I still make a fuss.

At night I wake up at midnight
and I make a fuss always.

At night I sleep because the moon
makes me sleep.

Olsi Mataj (7)
Merlin Primary School, Bromley

Snow

Snow is cool, snow is wicked
Snow is fun, snow is cold.
Snow is better than you, thick snow is good.
Snow is snowballs, snow is white.
Snow is snow, snow is slippery.
Snow is here, snow blocks the drain.
Snow makes the birds go away,
Snow is brill.

Hayden Causton (7)
Merlin Primary School, Bromley

School

At school I get crazy at football
At school I fall in water
At school I cry
At school in the morning I sleep
At school I get angry
At school I play
At school when it rains I never get to play
At school I like learning.

Jonathan Faonson (7)
Merlin Primary School, Bromley

When I

When I go to sleep I see Little Bo Peep
When I wake up in the morning I see the day is dawning
When I eat my dinner I feel a lot thinner
I play with my toys and then I go and see the boys.
We go to the park to have a lark.
Mummy comes along to see how we are doing and calls us
                                                           in for tea.

Leighan Hunt (7)
Northumberland Heath Primary School, Erith

Down At The Market

Roll up, roll up, roll up,
Come and get your bags of sweets.
Jelly babies, wine gums, teddy bears,
All at a low price, and yummy to eat.

Roll up, roll up, roll up,
Come and get your toys,
Barbie, Power Rangers, yo-yo and Spider-Man,
A selection for girls and boys.

Roll up, roll up, roll up,
Come and get your bags and cases,
Stripy, spotty, numbered and plain,
You need them when you go to places.

Roll up, roll up, roll up,
Come and get your fresh meat here,
Pork chops, lamb chops, mince and beef,
There won't be a single tear.

Roll up, roll up, roll up
Come and get your fast growing flowers,
Roses, daisies, sunflowers and tulips
You can put them anywhere, even on top of towers.

Roll up, roll up, roll up
Come and get your fruit and veg,
Apples, pears, cauliflower and lettuce,
Put them in your meal or have them on the edge.

Roll up, roll up, roll up,
Come and get your top quality shoe
Trainers, slippers, boots and wellies
You'll be so happy your friends might want a pair too.

Roll up, roll up, roll up,
Come and get your hair scrunchies and toggles,
Beige, red, blue and green
Buy five and get a free pair of goggles.

Rebecca Paul (8)
Northumberland Heath Primary School, Erith

My Family

Family life can be really great
I have a wonderful Mum
Who's just like my mate!
My sister is cool, she's loving
And fun
She helps me out when things
Need to be done.

As for my dad he's funny and
Mad
He's also very cuddly even when
I'm bad
My brother is older and growing up fast
He enjoys playing football
And did gymnastics in the past.

In our house most of the time
We all get along
And my sister and I
Enjoy a little song
All in all family life is very good
As long as the children do as they should.

Zoe Fortune (11)
Northumberland Heath Primary School, Erith

Valentine's Day

Roses are red, violets are blue
Sugar is sweet and so are you.
A light bulb is hot
But you are sweet
All the time you eat wheat.

Leia Elliott (8)
Northumberland Heath Primary School, Erith

My Special Friend

My special friend I used to love,
Has now gone to the clouds above.
Her eyes would glisten in the night
It was a truly magnificent sight.

She would put her head upon my knee
I'd look at her and she'd look back at me.
Her nose was cold and sometimes wet,
She was my dearest loving pet.

Sometimes she would make me laugh,
Often she would act quite daft.
One thing she loved was to go to the park,
Even though I found it scary and dark.

I think of her almost every day,
There's so much I would like to say
If she could have a second chance,
I would show my joy in a joyful dance.

I love my dog, she was my friend
All my love I would like to send
I can't play with her she has gone away,
But I will be with her again one day.

Harry Rogers (11)
Northumberland Heath Primary School, Erith

My Family

My dad is running wild
He is acting like a child.
But mostly he
Only stops for me,
And also his manners are mild!

My mum is going mad,
And insane might I add!
She's going to blow!
And it'll fly out our window,
Plus I'm sure it will smell bad.

Jasmin is cool,
Tanya thinks I'm a fool,
Anita eats sweets,
But not all of her meat,
And they are all at school.

I am by far the best!
I'm energetic and never rest,
I'm amazingly pretty,
And remarkably witty,
But don't always do well on my tests!

Shaan Sangha (10)
Northumberland Heath Primary School, Erith

The Love Letter

Dear my dearest love,
Your eyes make me twinkle like the stars above.
When I see you I begin to shake,
You seem to think my love is fake.

When I am not with you, I miss you so
But my love for you will always show.
With little things I do and say,
My heart with you will always stay.

My passion for you grows by the hour,
Your lips are as beautiful as a flower.
You thought there was no I in me,
I hope together we will always be.

A future I can see for us,
Is full of laughter, fun and love.
Forever and always we will stand,
Side by side on golden sand.

When old age comes I will love you still,
A lifetime's dreams will be for filled,
To have spent my life with my one true love,
Is more than I could ever dream of.

Nicholas Hutchinson (11)
Northumberland Heath Primary School, Erith

Apples

You have an apple, but what kind?
You need to make up your mind!
Is it going to be red or green?
You can't judge really until you have seen.
What has the supermarket got in store?
Or what lies on the orchard floor?

A walk in the orchard on a hot sunny day
Is cheerful enough to make anyone gay.
I reach up high into the trees
Paying lots of attention to mind the bees!
Busy buzzing about their work,
Never intending to ever hurt.

As I bite into the apple I crunch
Apples are extremely delicious to munch.
The first bite reveals a juicy white inside
Another bite deeper I can confide
Lots of tiny brown pips in the core
Which scatter upon the orchard floor.

The cycle begins again as the pips take root
Be careful not to stand on one with your boot!
The growth of an apple tree takes many years
Will I still be here when the apples appear?
My children walk through pastures new,
Is that my apple tree that I once grew?

Hannah Dowsett (11)
Northumberland Heath Primary School, Erith

My Special Friend

I have a very special friend,
her name is Lucy-Jo.
I tell her all about myself
about my friends and foes.

She listens so intently
to what I have to say
she's there for me by day and night
and never does complain.

I love my little friend
she doesn't answer back
and when I'm feeling all upset,
she's there to take the rap.

We cuddle up at bedtime
she sleeps upon my pillow
my dearest friend, sweet Lucy-Jo
my all time favourite hero.

I bet you all think she's just a friend
that's just like any other
but let me tell you that Lucy-Jo
is my mum, my dad, my sisters and brothers
all rolled into one.

Who is she?
She is my dolly of course.

Hollie Love (8)
Northumberland Heath Primary School, Erith

The Fight

Whatever I do I will not age
It will drive me into a complete rage.
So I try to keep calm
So you better keep me under a charm.

I'm a man of great strength
And I'll go to any length
To prove I can do it
With all my wits to it.

I will see you
And I will fight you.
My chest is feeling tight
I'm getting ready to fight.

I'll see you later
I'll be in a crater
Have a wish for seven balls
And you will get free calls.

Come with me
And you will see
Fusion with trunks and Goten
That will make Gotex.

Despite all my rage
I'm still just a rat in a cage . . .
Then someone will say,
'What is lost can never be saved . . .'

Joe Davies (11)
Northumberland Heath Primary School, Erith

The Thick White Blanket

As the cold whisper of the cold wind cried,
The weather catastrophe arised,
The soft snowflakes, jewelled grass,
Snow had justified weather, as cold would never pass.

The puzzled children jumped with glee,
While I stood there, cold and lonely whilst shivers showered me,
A spine tingling fright of cold shot down,
My heart cannot resist; but pound.

Horrifying questions whizzed through my mind,
What if my parents would not be able to see me or find!
My toes were numb and stood as still as a stationed car;
I would surely not be able to travel far.

I shook my head in disbelief,
I muttered and tried to let out a sigh of relief.
I hated the cold, breezy snow,
And the giant big wind roar.

My heart boiled with steam, anger and rage,
I wish the snow were something that could turn over like a page.
Due to the cold, the books I held would no longer hold,
My face was red-hot with anger, as my body went cold.

My emotions grew they were soon to explode,
My tears jumped down; I wish it had never showed!
Everyone loved the famous, thick, white snow - all but me,
Like the others, I wish I could show a great quantity of glee.

I suddenly felt connection between the snows!
I then clambered to touch and then down low.
The soft, white, cold feeling filled my heart with joy,
Was that the snow I'd once hated with no appreciation at all?

Latisha Oozageer (10)
Northumberland Heath Primary School, Erith

Boring Bob

When boring Bob
Ever looked for a job,
They always end up saying:
'No! Because I'll only end up paying!'
So he never earns any money,
That's why his nose is always runny.
His clothes are tight,
He's dull not bright,
He sleeps on the floor,
And always utters the English law!
He doesn't eat any food,
And he can't say cool dude.
He's very stupid and boring,
But most of the time he's drawing!
He eats so many bugs,
That's why he never gets hugs!
The stupid man,
Can't cook in a pan!
He plays in dirt,
And rips his shirt!
He laughs like a pig,
And he's very, very *big!*
Blisters on his face,
Always loves to chase!
Then he starts to cry,
And you can't pass by,
He asks for his mummy,
And wants to fill his tummy,
Then he sees you . . .
And goes, 'Boo hoo.'

Sharonpreet Sadhra (9)
Northumberland Heath Primary School, Erith

Monsters

When the vampires appear
You'll quickly want to disappear
When the ghosts quiver
It would make you shake and shiver
Down your spine
Like an electric line
Don't worry you'll be fine.

When it's the night for the witches
They won't let it go with any hitches
But when it's the wizard's time to play
All they do is lay.
Although the gnomes look still
They're not afraid to kill
And even the devil with its spear
Will shake you with fear.
Not to mention the scary ghouls
Who lurk around school halls
Although we know zombies are dead
It does not stop them taking your head.

The headless horseman can drive you mad
So you will be very sad
We all know werewolves bite
But only during the night

That's all the monsters you will know
So keep your head down and stay low
Or you'll end you your own foe
So when you watch the sun go down
Go and buy the Baskervilles hound
Or you'll be killed before you make a sound
So keep your head to the ground.

Hayley Morris (11)
Northumberland Heath Primary School, Erith

What My Mum Says

When I'm in the car,
Mum says I'm a star,
When I start to cry,
Mum sings me a lullaby.
When I'm in the shower,
Mum says I've got the power.
When I want to dive,
Mum gives me a high five.
When I'm in the bath,
She says you're always having a laugh.
When I eat a carrot,
Mum say's you'll be a parrot.
When I'm at the seaside,
She says watch the tide.
When I'm a feeling sick,
Mum says have first pick.
When I'm very steady,
Mum gives me a teddy.
When I want my bunny,
Mum says I'm funny.
When I eat a chip,
Mum says have a kip.
When I drink juice,
Mum says are your trousers loose?
When I lose my pen
Mum says feed the hen.
When I'm playing dead
Mum says go to bed.
If I broke a jug,
Mum says give me a hug.

Jaspreet Sadhra (8)
Northumberland Heath Primary School, Erith

The Knights Of Morcia

The Knights of Morcia want the title 'Great Knight'.
So then they have to be brave and fight.

There's dashing Sir Jayko, his strength is his speed,
In the great tournament his sword he will need.

There's also Sir Santis, the strongest of all,
If you compare his size, it's quite tall.

Next up is Danju, very clever and wise.
In all his battles he has won first prize.

Last of all there's Rascus, the joker of the four.
But his enemies aren't laughing when he rides out to war.

Four knights all with different skills trying to win,
The seventh moon is rising, let the battle now begin.

Richard Masheder (8)
Northumberland Heath Primary School, Erith

The Cat The Dog And The Frog

There was a fat cat,
That sat on a red mat.
Eating his tea
With Harry and me.

There was a giant frog,
Sitting on a wet log.
Drinking cold water,
From the Malta.

The cat and the frog,
Were friends with a dog.
Who ate their dinner
And was onto a winner.

Georgina Stock (8)
Northumberland Heath Primary School, Erith

The Best Team In The World

There is an Arsenal team
Who always play like a dream
Last week they played Man U
And they won the game 3-2.
So now we are in top spot
And we play to stay until we drop
Piers and Bergkamp pass the ball,
Campbell, Vieira and Henry say, 'All for one and one for all.'

Arsenal's goalie is Jans Leighan
He's our No 1 goalie
He always saves them
Our players stay on their feet
And give our fans such a treat.

I'll practice my dribbling and be a good runner
So I'll stay on track to become a good gunner.

Daniel Page (7)
Northumberland Heath Primary School, Erith

Bob

I know a man called Bob
And he had a fantastic job
His hobby is to play football
Or instead baseball.

He is a very nice man
And he has a friend called Dan
Bob would like to be in a band one day
But he doesn't know how to play.

Bob was a lonely man
But he also had a friend called Ann
He had a dog called Pob
And that's a story about Bob.

John Boswell (10)
Northumberland Heath Primary School, Erith

Australia

Australia is hot,
They get tourists quite a lot
Never have a cold day
If they did they would run away.
There's a main city called Sydney
A great fan of steak and kidney
Go and visit Sydney Opera House
It's better than any old green house.
You might see the Minogues
Or even go to one of their shows.
Learn how to surf
Play hockey on nice turf
I say, 'G'day'
Hope you enjoy your Australian holiday!

Katie Hookway (11)
Northumberland Heath Primary School, Erith

My Labrador, Pepsi

My dog is the colour of coal, with big brown eyes that shine like gold
A big wet nose that likes to sniff
But if she rolls in something, smelly, oh dear does she whiff
You can't stay angry with her for long
Even if she does pong
Her head tilts and her eyes look sad
It makes me feel really bad
She is as greedy as can be
And if she could she would eat a tree
But I love her all the same
She is the dog for me.

Lilly Webb (8)
Northumberland Heath Primary School, Erith

War No More

War broke out
The world seemed red.
Loves were lost
And people paid the cost.

Lost limbs, broken spirits
Hearts could not prevail.
There was no hope
And nature could not cope.

But victory came at last
And loves came home to rest
Cuddles and kisses all around
And peace was found.

Julian Bates (10)
Northumberland Heath Primary School, Erith

Cat's Eyes

There's a girl in my class called Kyes,
She has these really green eyes,
Last night I was walking in the garden,
I heard a hiss, I beg your pardon.
I thought it was Dad,
He's not that mad!
Then in a gap in the wall,
I saw two eyes like Kyes from school.
I think she turns into a cat at night,
Last night she really gave me a fright!

Sarah Beale (10)
Northumberland Heath Primary School, Erith

My Dream Man

The smoke rose from the romantic surprise
It's the meal of my dreams
Well that's how it seemed.

I didn't eat it straight away
Instead I sat down and said a prayer
The prayer for my man and me
Prayed for the future and following dreams.

After a special night I went home
Thinking of his house of Rome
It was like the Italy town
It wasn't like feeling upset or down.

Instead I feel happy and glad
Glad that I have my dream man
I know that he's the one.

Natasha Gibbons (9)
Royal Alexandra & Albert School, Reigate

Fairy Tale

Once Shrek heard a bark
And then he saw a spark
He walked into the dark
And there was Noah's Ark.

Shrek found some magic
And it was very, very tragic.
He came across a fairy
Whose knees were very hairy.

The fairy was hairy
Her name was Mary
She came across a hare
Whose name was Claire.

Franny Townsend (8)
Royal Alexandra & Albert School, Reigate

Fairy Tale Rhymes

There once was an ogre called Shrek
His garden was a deck
He woke up a beautiful princess
And she thought his room was a mess.

His room was a mess
So he covered it in a dress
The princess saw a prince
So they went off eating mince.

Shrek saw a spark
So he went back in his ark
He looked outside and saw an elf
And the elf just cared about himself.

Shrek went in the park
And saw a statue of a shark
He screamed with fright
To see such a sight.

Chelsea Metcalfe (9)
Royal Alexandra & Albert School, Reigate

I Met An Old Man

I met an old man
Whose name was Dan
Who was a big fan
Of Jackie Chan
And then he met a man
Called Stan
Who also knew Jackie Chan.
Then Stan went crazy
Who met a girl called Mazy
And he picked her a daisy
Ten years later he got lazy
And said goodbye to Mazy.

Jack Hart (9)
Royal Alexandra & Albert School, Reigate

Wish Upon A Star

As I go to bed I see a shiny image
Looking back at me as it flickers
In the sky I wish that I could fly up high
As it twinkles in the sky
I wish this feeling will never die.

Suddenly I notice my love up above
Calling to me as he dances and prances
I fly up high to the sky to be with my love up above
As I wish upon a star
I notice what the wonders are.

Love is the same as liking something lots
It could be chocolates, roses or not
When you're alone and feeling blue
Love is there to guide you through.

Anji Baba-Ahmed (10)
Royal Alexandra & Albert School, Reigate

Bullying

Bullying is a bruise
A bruise in your heart
You can't control it
No you can't.

When you're alone
You're scared if it comes
No one protects you
You're the only one.

Let's hope you learn
Your lesson today
So all we hope
That today is the day.

Shannon Chiverton (10)
Royal Alexandra & Albert School, Reigate

The Girl And The Well

There once was a girl
Who wore a romantic pearl,
When she rings the bell
Up comes a well,
She heard a moan,
Then a groan
It was coming from the well,
The girl looked down, there was a damp smell.

She ran to her house,
And saw a little mouse,
She went to get a rope
But lost her hope,
She pulled him up,
And tried to smarten him up.

When he got older,
He became a soldier
They got happily married,
And she got carried
They had little kids
Who were beautiful little kids.

Amy Broad (10)
Royal Alexandra & Albert School, Reigate

Over The Rainbow

Over the rainbow is a young girl
With miniature pink pigtails
Over the rainbow is an expensive white pearl
Hiding in a cloud waiting to drop.

Over the rainbow is a thick gold book
Full of surprises to find out too
Over the rainbow is a small dog
They took from the RSPCA as a pet.

Laura Cogger (10)
Royal Alexandra & Albert School, Reigate

Love

There was a girl
Who was going to get married
She was so pretty
You could imagine her eye
On a golden carriage!

She says tomorrow's the day
For my wedding
I'm really nervous
I'm really sweating
Tomorrow my love I say how I feel
Then later that day we're having a romantic meal
See you chow!

Now darling I say how I feel
And then we go out for a romantic meal.
Now remember when yesterday I said chow
Well today I stand up and say my vow
Now forever on I say how I feel
I will love you forever my heart will seal with love
With hope, with beauty
I hope you love one of us all
I hope especially it's me
I love you everybody, I love you all
But especially my man who is really cool.

Shanice Gibbons (9)
Royal Alexandra & Albert School, Reigate

Day Haiku

The sun is awake
The butterfly flutters by
The birds sing their song.

Ellie Drummey (9)
Royal Alexandra & Albert School, Reigate

Fairy Tale Poem

Fairies shine like wine
They are good unlike the Devil
Whose secret nickname is Neville.

There was once a fairy called Mary
Who was very, very hairy.
But Mary had a pet canary
Who was very, very scary.

A hairy troll guards a scroll
With his friend Mr Mole
Who has a bowl of cherries
And who has the spell for merry berries.

Giants have big bums
Giants have numb thumbs
Giants have lots of money
And giants have small bunnies.

There was once a genie
Who was very teeny
Who also lived in a tin can
With a very fat old man.

Thomas James (9)
Royal Alexandra & Albert School, Reigate

Horses

Horses are fast
They trot, canter and gallop
I like to ride them.

Nadia Fowler (9)
Royal Alexandra & Albert School, Reigate

Woodland

In the woodland, squirrels climb
Birds fly looking for food
Mice scurry about collecting berries
Hedgehogs wake up in spring.

In the woodland you find flowers
Tulips are yellow, red and orange
Daffodils open their heads
Forget-me-nots as blue as blue.

In the woodland it is peaceful
Only the sounds of leaves rustling
And water trickling in the stream
Quiet is the woodland.

In the woodland different trees grow
Sycamore, Chestnut, are kinds of trees
Beech and Ash grow in woods and
Oak the oldest of all, grows in the heart
Of the *woodland!*

Elizabeth Kendra (9)
Royal Alexandra & Albert School, Reigate

The Weather!

That rain that falls from way up high
Why must such things come from the sky?
The depression from all these people mound,
Why must it become non-existent when it hits the ground?

That sun that shines from way up high,
You can see that gentle free dove fly,
That happiness that spreads all around
Will come even though the sun doesn't make a sound.

Laura Holmes (10)
Royal Alexandra & Albert School, Reigate

Once Upon A Time

Once upon a time
very long ago
in a land far away
where the sun is bright
and the clouds are white
the trees bend and sway.

Once upon a time
not so long ago
in that happy land far away
running in the sands
two children holding hands
singing their cares away.

Once upon a time
not that long ago
I flew to the land far away
I ran in the sands
waving my hands
singing my cares away.

Once upon a time
a little while ago
in the beautiful land far away
for a great many years
through laughter and fears
I lived in the land far away.

Yasmin Anderson (8)
Royal Alexandra & Albert School, Reigate

Fairy Tale Poem

Shrek was an ogre
He wore a toga
Shrek was big and scary
Shrek was very hairy.

There once was an elf
Who kept himself to himself
The elf was very tiny
In the dark he looked all shiny.

The troll was big and fat
And he had a blue hat
The troll was big he could not walk
He was so quiet you could not hardly hear him talk.

There once was a fairy and in her eye she has a spark
She's nice through the day and the dark.
She lives in a tree
That's covered with lots of bark.

Charlotte Price (9)
Royal Alexandra & Albert School, Reigate

About An Old Man

This old man is not life
He always wears a white coat.

He makes people happy
Everyone loves him.

But someone wants to kill him
They try every way but they can't kill him. Why?
Because he gets super power.

He dies for us
His blood cleans our thoughts.

But three days he comes back to Earth.

Vincent Chiu (10)
Royal Alexandra & Albert School, Reigate

Fairy Tales

I went to the wood
I wore a hood
I met a boy called Robin Hood
Then he took me to a different wood.

We came across a stream
Of which rays of light beam
The stream was like
A piece of cream.

I saw a toad jump over
Then suddenly I saw a clover
The clover had a four leaf
Which felt like a pair of teeth.

It looked really nice
So I cooked it with a touch of rice
I thought I should sell it for a really cheap price
So I sold it for the price of a box of rice.

Jack Hawkes (9)
Royal Alexandra & Albert School, Reigate

Night

I know a man called Ned
Who has a king-sized bed.
He thinks he sees sharks
and strange things in the dark.
When children scream
It's because of a scary dream.
When they're trying to sleep
All they here is a big *beep!*

    That's the story of night.

Madelaine Hart (9)
Royal Alexandra & Albert School, Reigate

Fairy Tale Poem

I once saw a witch
Putting someone in a ditch
She said, 'Give me the gold,'
I said, 'No it's been sold.'

We bumped into a genie
Who was quite teeny
He said, 'Where's the gold?'
She said, 'It's been sold.'

They all bumped into a troll
He had his foot stuck down a hole
Then the troll said, 'Give me the gold'
She said, 'It's been sold.'

Then they all saw Jack
They laughed at him when he had his smack
He said, 'I want the gold!'
'For heaven's sake it's been sold.'

They came across a book of magic
They knew the results would be tragic
They tried to use the book to make gold
But they just didn't understand that the gold was sold.

Amy-Louise Ralph (9)
Royal Alexandra & Albert School, Reigate

Sally The Horse

She has a brown coat
Sometimes Nadia rides her
She jumps quietly.

Jessie Sharp (9)
Royal Alexandra & Albert School, Reigate

Fairy Tale

Once there was a fairy
Who had a yellow canary
She took him to see an elf
Who enjoyed a great deal of wealth.

When the canary met Jack
He gave him a pat on the back
He was always having fun
Enjoying the money he had won!

When all of a sudden there was a giant
Who was very silent
Who took the money
That was from Sonny.

Then a devil
Was on a level
There was a shark
On a piece of bark.

Then awoke Shrek
Who found himself in a wreck
And saw a ray of sunshine
That was reflected off a glass of wine.

Harry Skinner (9)
Royal Alexandra & Albert School, Reigate

Paris Haiku

Paris is my home
I love the Eiffel Tower
Disneyland is cool!

Coralie Glomaud (9)
Royal Alexandra & Albert School, Reigate

Fairy Tales

There once were some bears
In their house they had chairs
The mummy bear met a boy
And his name was Troy.

Troy was very nice
But you have to think twice
He was very hairy
As well as mummy bear Mary.

They were very happy
Except they had to change the baby's nappy
But they were still mates
But then they went on a date.

They went on four dates
But they were still mates
But one day Troy said, 'I love you'
What about Mary I bet her that's new.

Mary said, 'I love you too
But I am still in love with Hugh.'
They were very happy
But they still had to change the baby's nappy.

Faye Kennesion (8)
Royal Alexandra & Albert School, Reigate

Nature

Children playing in the sun
running about and having fun.

Waving in the nice, cool breeze
are a bunch of lovely trees.

People watering all the flowers
as they grow with mighty powers.

Russell Gills (8)
Royal Alexandra & Albert School, Reigate

Fairy Tale Poem

There was a wolf
And he went North
He said, 'Goodbye,' to the dragon
So the dragon went off with the wagon.

There was a joker
Who saw a smoker
And went to say, 'Bug off'
But the smoker was a moth.

There was a king
With a diamond ring
And he gave it to a troll
But Mr Troll put it in a bowl.

The fat goblin
Was really wobbling
And he went to say, 'I'm off
With some candyfloss.'

A fairy light
Flew through the night
And waved her magic wand
And crashed into a pond.

Oliver Phillips (8)
Royal Alexandra & Albert School, Reigate

Car

Monday - dead battery
Tuesday - new battery
Wednesday - starting to drive
Thursday - driving too fast
Friday - free ride in a police car.

Raphaelson Aghahan (9)
Royal Alexandra & Albert School, Reigate

Darkness

Her mother tucked her into bed
And her head sank into the pillow
And her eyes began to close.

She drifted into a darkness
Of discomfort and devastation
And it seemed so real to her.

A crazed horse came
Running everywhere
And then it was gone.

It had disappeared
And then the world started turning
And a strong wind shocked her.

After that everything faded away
Into a warmth and pale light
Which made her think of her bedroom.

And then she realised what it was
It was her room
And then she knew it had all been a dream.

Ana Whittock (10)
Royal Alexandra & Albert School, Reigate

The Ship

We built a ship upon the stairs
All made of the back bedroom chairs
And filled with pillows
To go sailing the Irish seas.

We sailed along for days and days
And had the very best of plays
But Naomi fell out and hurt her knee
So there was no one left but me.

Jacob McQuillan (10)
St Joseph's RC Primary School, Redhill

My Gingerbread Man

I bought myself a gingerbread man,
That was bigger than my dog,
Off it jumped from the table and ran,
Out into the thick misty fog!

I called for him but he didn't come,
So I had to go and look for him,
I felt like his mum,
I soon found him floating on a log in a lake,
His face looked tired,
Was he asleep or awake?
I shook him hard but he did not budge,
He was like a still orange figure,
Like a piece of fudge!

I gave him up for dead,
And laid him in my bed,
My poor dead gingerbread man,
That I was going to eat,
I told him that I was his biggest fan,
But he was larger than my feet!

Florence Pettet (10)
St Joseph's RC Primary School, Redhill

My Friends

My friends are always there for me,
And so am I for them,
We stick together like honey in a beehive
Playing games, having fun and building dens!

I suppose we're all like five petals
Held together on a flower,
A bit like a packet of sweets,
Some plain, some sweet but none sour!

Fiona Quinn (10)
St Joseph's RC Primary School, Redhill

When The Raindrops Fall

When the raindrops fall a sort of magic begins to grow.

When the raindrops fall there's a sort of power which
Contains a beautiful sunny day.

When the raindrops fall a rainbow
Begins to show.

When the raindrops fall a kind of feeling begins
To grow.

When the raindrops fall a rainbow sparkles
Down on you.

Zoe-Ann Savage (10)
St Joseph's RC Primary School, Redhill

Holidays

Off we go on a holiday,
But we're still extremely far away!
Further away from home we go
The local language we don't know!
The sun looks like a ball of fire
As the temperature rises higher and higher!
I'm happy to be here, as there's no school,
I'll be glad to go for a dip in the pool!
I'm missing home quite a lot,
But I'm missing school, definitely not!
As we go for a picnic in the sun,
All to be had is fun, fun, fun!

Tobin Jardine (10)
St Joseph's RC Primary School, Redhill

My Short Life

I was born in '93
The first thing I did was to have a wee.
My mum and dad should have been happy
However I wasn't wearing a nappy.

It was my first trip at the age of two,
We all went off to London Zoo.
The journey in the car was ever so long,
Then we smelt a familiar pong!

At the age of four I went to school
In my uniform I looked rather cool.
There I made friends with Matthew Carter,
Because he caused a lot of laughter.

I made friends with Josh at the age of six,
Between us we caused a lot of tricks.
Football was our favourite game,
And all the others felt the same.

When I was at the age of eight,
I became regularly late!
It was so hard to get out of my bed,
Having to lift my fact-filled head.

Now I've reached the age of ten,
Us boys turning into trendy young men.
I've been selected for the school football team,
To win the cup is my future dream!

Thomas Rowntree (10)
St Joseph's RC Primary School, Redhill

My School Is Great

Schools are boring as most people say,
But I think my school is great.
Today was the best day ever,
Except that my best friend was late.

At half past ten I went out to play
And the teacher blew her whistle.
It's time for fun, it's time for games,
And she gave us all a water pistol.

My friend turned up, the water fight began,
She got soaked by the unruly crowd
She got enormously wet
So she screamed so very loud.

The teacher came up and said, 'Don't be silly,'
She said 'It's only a game.'
She gave my friend a water pistol too,
So she could do the same.

Natasha Jardine (10)
St Joseph's RC Primary School, Redhill

School's Out

S chool's dismissed, 'Hip hooray!'
C ool! It is the holidays
H appy days having fun
O n the beach and in the sun
O h, how great it can be
L arking around in the sea
S ix weeks off! No school work

O h that really is a perk
U p with fun, down with school
T aking time off is our rule.

Jack Dunne (9)
St Joseph's RC Primary School, Redhill

Cinderella

My sisters think they are so smart
Not as in good at maths, English or art,
But they think they are so sneaky
They want me to cry 'Oh you're so creepy!'
Fat chance of that!
I'd rather be knocked in the face, splat!
It was just the other day
I tried to get into my room but they blocked my way.
I peeped over their shoulders,
And two packs of itching powder stood out like huge boulders.
I acted like I'd not seen it
But I'd already thought of a plan that would be a smash hit.
As quick as a flash I made a dash,
Towards my knicker drawer,
'This will make them itch until their skin is red raw!'
I said to myself as I swapped our knickers roun'
'Tomorrow they will look like clowns!'
The next day they really did look daft
Whilst they scratched and scratched I laughed.

Katie Dowds (10)
St Joseph's RC Primary School, Redhill

My Family

M y family's a good one
Y ou should have one too.

F un and cool wherever we go,
A nd great places we've been
M um, Dad, Chris and me
I n the car
L aughing away
Y ou don't know what you're missing.

Emma Lewis (9)
St Joseph's RC Primary School, Redhill

The Cat Named Lynn

There once was a beautiful cat
Who was known for wearing a hat
Her name was Lynn
But was as skinny as a pin
And that was that!

Until one day she ate too much fat
So ended up as a back street cat.

Lynn was lonely and sad
She had not meant to be so bad.
She decided to stop eating from bins
In a few weeks she began to be thin.

Everybody wanted her return
Because there was so much concern,
She ran back to the house
As a reward she was given a mouse!

Night came fast
She was home at last
She started to purr
As she licked her fur
She fell fast asleep
Without a peep.

On her head was her hat
And that was the end of that!

Isabella Wynn (10)
St Joseph's RC Primary School, Redhill

Ghandi

There was an old man called Ghandi
Who went into a pub for a shandy
With a loin cloth he wiped up the froth,
The barmaid said, 'Blimey! That's handy.'

Hannah Jobbins-Hone (10)
St Joseph's RC Primary School, Redhill

The FFF Poem
(Football Fun Friendship)

F ootball at school is fun because I play for the team
O ften I play with my friends as well
O r the older years
T he weekend is also fun
B ecause I play for Horley Town
A nd I have a lot of friends there
L ots of practice is done on Saturday
L astly I play a match on Sunday.

Jamie Wornham (10)
St Joseph's RC Primary School, Redhill

Poppy

Poppy is a kitten who likes to play with mittens
She pulls at the stitch but that is only one trick.

She sits on her mat with the name Cat,
She cleans her fur with a big loud purr.

She eats her lunch with a munch and crunch,
And licks the dish she loves her fish!

Ruth Connolly (9)
St Joseph's RC Primary School, Redhill

My Baby Brother

J oe is his name, fun is his game
O nly one baby brother, there is no other
E very day he loves to play, no matter what the weather

J ust one smile seems to beam for a mile
O ne of a kind is my Joe
E ven strangers stop and say, 'Oh! What a beautiful baby.'

Joshua Richards (9)
St Joseph's RC Primary School, Redhill

My Favourite Things

My name is Keelan Twomey
And I'd like to share with you
All my very favourite things
I like to see and do.

I love to go on aeroplanes
And jet off somewhere hot
Sun and sea and ice cream
And a day trip on a yacht.

I love to watch old steam trains
Chugging on old lines
Or hit a golf ball sure and straight
With club or woods or irons.

My nannies and my grandad
And all my family
My friends at school and teachers
All mean the world to me.

My favourite food is chocolate
And sticky gooey sweets
But Mum says I can't eat them
Or else I'll need false teeth.

My favourite meal is breakfast
With slices of hot buttered toast
Cereal, cold milk, tea and juice
Are what I like the most.

I really like computer games
And riding on my bike
Or scooting on my scooter
Or going on a hike.

My favourite things, the list's so long
I really could go on and on.

Keelan Twomey (9)
St Joseph's RC Primary School, Redhill

Prison

Staring at these four grey walls,
Walking through these long dark halls.
Nowhere to look and nowhere to run,
I only blame myself, all this for fun.
Hearing the noise and knowing the days,
Old men screaming, stuck in their ways.

The food is bad, it makes me ill
I only eat lunch, just to feel chilled.
Sundays are roast with burnt gravy,
Chef makes the peas, all mushy and wavy.
I need to behave I want to go home,
Because at this time I feel so alone.

If only I had not been so bad,
Just think of all the things I could have had.
I could walk in fields and play anytime,
Instead of just waiting in line.
I will never do anything wrong again,
I don't want to live with a thousand men.

Mathew Samuel (9)
St Joseph's RC Primary School, Redhill

My Pet Cat

My pet cat is ginger,
You should feel his soft fur.

Pets are really brilliant
Even if you have to clean them out!
Tara has a pet dog.

Cats come in all different colours, shapes and sizes
A day or two ago someone came to see my pet,
                              called Grindilow,
They said that he is beautiful, they said that about
My pet cat.

Sophie Stratfull (9)
St Joseph's RC Primary School, Redhill

Midsummer Wanderer

No lights all around,
No lights anywhere,
Black as night
She wanders round
Looking for something
She casts a spell
A wicked spell
And aims at a woodland close by.
Screams and shouts from everyone,
As the spell hits the ground,
The only laugh in the town
Came from she.
The wicked witch
Upon a town that night.

Rebecca Rogers (10)
St Joseph's RC Primary School, Redhill

My Fish

I call my goldfish Bunny
He is very funny
He chews seaweed all night
And looks quite a fright!

His best friend is Hoppip
Who hasn't quite got it!
And there's Big Barry
Who is twins with Little Larry.

They're all my little fishes
Shaped like dishes!
In my room
Under the broom!

Kate Stebbings (10)
St Joseph's RC Primary School, Redhill

My Guitar And Me

My name is Stephen Murphy
I'm quite a clever boy
Cos when I play on my guitar
It brings me so much joy.

I strum the strings and play a tune
That makes my family proud
But when I play The Chilli Peppers
I'm told that's far too loud.

I nearly make the windows break
While practising my chords
The neighbours bang loudly on the walls
And jump on their floorboards.

But I am actually not so bad
They've asked me on the telly
To play alongside someone cool
An elephant called Nelly.

One day I'll play on Top of the Pops
With my new hit 'Stephen's Mum!'
I'll rock and roll and twist and shake
And even play my drum.

So remember when I'm famous
I will play it just for laughs
And when I'm leaving Planet Hollywood
Please ask for autographs.

But really it was all a dream
I really am quite poor
So sign me up The Chilli Peppers
And I'll play on your next tour.

Stephen Murphy (9)
St Joseph's RC Primary School, Redhill

Patrick's Hat-Trick

There was a young striker called Patrick
Whose efforts on the field were slapstick
He practised until
He almost felt ill
But next game he scored his first hat-trick!

When he was older,
And the days felt colder
He joined a professional team
And one of the matches it started to seem
That Patrick
Would score one more hat-trick!

The score was two all
He was facing a wall
All eyes were focused on Patrick
When the free kick he took
The stadium shook
For Patrick had scored one more hat-trick!

Alexander Stearn (10)
St Joseph's RC Primary School, Redhill

Tennis Mayhem

T ortoises play it slowly
E skimos use snow shoes
N ewts are nifty with their tails
N omads never stay long enough to finish a match
I ron Age champs whacked iron balls
S lippery snakes serve slimy shots.

C rafty crabs pinch a point
O ctopuses with eight rackets are hard to beat,
U nderwater creatures volley with shells
R eindeers rain off every match
T ell the coach I'm not so bad after all!

Alex Ramsden (9)
St Joseph's RC Primary School, Redhill

My Cat Called Pepper

Pepper is a small tabby cat,
He dances and he prances, he likes doing that
Pepper runs and plays with a red ball of string
My Pepper plays with everything.
My cat has friends and goes out to play,
He loves it when it's a nice sunny day.
He runs around the garden and climbs up the trees
He often falls off, clinging onto the leaves.
Sometimes he catches a bird or a mouse and leaves them as presents around our house.
When he gets tired he jumps at the doors and through the letterbox he puts his paws.
When it's late and he's tired he's out like a light although sometimes he's naughty and stays out all night.

Daniel Sammut (9)
St Joseph's RC Primary School, Redhill

The Cricket Match

I walk out onto the pitch, my bat in hand
With my pads big and thick,
There they are ready to bowl quite quick
I smash the ball up into the air,
The crowd stands up and claps and cheers
Six more runs and the score is near.
But then another six is sent into the air,
And the batsman's really showing his flair.
The sun is shining in the sky
Only one more over to go.
Six more runs that's all we need,
I flash my bat, I did the deed.
Cheering, shouting, singing and dancing
We're all happy, let's keep on prancing.

Harry Curran (9)
St Joseph's RC Primary School, Redhill

Our Puppy

We are getting a puppy next week,
And I am finding it hard to sleep,
He has furry white paws and little black claws
And we are bringing him home to keep.

I will teach him to jump up and down
And chase me around and around
I will scratch his belly
While we watch the telly
And we will both fall asleep safe and sound.

I will take him for walks in the park,
And he will run very fast and bark.
He will chase the rabbits
As one of his habits
But he will not be afraid of the dark.

My puppy will chew lots of toys
And make a loud yappy noise.
His teeth will be sharp
Our chairs he might mark
But that will be one of his joys.

Eleanor Heaney (10)
St Joseph's RC Primary School, Redhill

My Teddy

I had a little teddy
and his name was Eddy
Eddy had a little tree
and a baby bumblebee.
One day he got stung
on his little tum.
He went to hide
then he cried
That's my little teddy
Eddy.

Joshua Leigh (10)
St Joseph's RC Primary School, Redhill

Chocolate

Chocolate is dreamy
A creamy treat
It melts like butter
And it makes your stomach flutter
There's dark, there's white and milk too
These are the varieties that I think will thrill you
They come in many shapes and sizes
And lots of colours too,
Practically any shop will do
Just for you.

And you can chew through a delicious Dairy Milk
Furthermore a packet of mouth-watering Minstrels
Meanwhile a gleaming Galaxy
And a bubbly Bounty
But last of all a twirling Twirl
And I bet your tummy aches!

Helen Redstone (10)
St Joseph's RC Primary School, Redhill

Teddy Bears

T eddy bears are soft and sweet
E ach of them are different
D ainty, little and tiny feet, (they are ones that I would like to meet)
D ry as a bone and very well groomed
Y ear by year they will never die.

B ears are the best to me
E veryone has to admit that bears are loveable and huggable
A ny bears are the best to me and I don't care what anyone says
R ough fur there are some kind. But not to me
S o there you go 'cause now we all know that teddy bears are the best.

Siobhan Robinson (10)
St Joseph's RC Primary School, Redhill

My Pet Tarantula

My pet tarantula is always on the move,
He bites every living thing,
He even bites Mum's wedding ring,
His name is Little Stanley,
He flees from tree to tree,
And when I call his little name . . .
He flees right back to me.

His favourite food is birds' eyes
Coiled in flattened snakes,
He also likes squeezed rat's blood
Over the furry skin.
For pudding he adores skinned men,
He especially likes the flesh,
He clears his plate completely not leaving a scrap in sight.

Grace Wilson (10)
St Joseph's RC Primary School, Redhill

Holidays

Holidays, holidays everywhere
Holidays, holidays anywhere
Up in the sky or down below
Anywhere you can go
England, France, America, Spain
Wherever you go you don't want rain
Swimming, skiing, fun matters too
Among the things that you can do
Into your suitcase quick take a look
Don't forget to take your book
Holidays, holidays must come to an end
So we can see our family and friends.

Emily Byrne (10)
St Joseph's RC Primary School, Redhill

Sunsets In Cornwall

Sunsets, sunsets, Cornwall sunsets,
Sun-sweet colours each dusk,
Red, orange and yellow,
Those are the colours of Cornwall sunsets.

Over the hills and above the trees,
The sunset starts to unlock with the keys.

It starts at 6.00 and ends at 7.00
Those are the hours of the sunsets in Heaven.

The sun is reflecting like a mirror
Over the calm seas
Then the sun is like a half cut orange
While the fire fades away.

Hannah Barnes (10)
St Joseph's RC Primary School, Redhill

Secrets

Whisper, whisper, from me to you
I put a spider in Luke's shoe
Stephen please don't tell
Can you keep this secret really well?

Stacie you won't guess what Luke has done
But don't tell or you'll ruin the fun
Jo put a spider in Luke's shoe,
Oh no, those shoes are really new.

Uh oh, I'd better tell you
That Jo put a spider in your shoe
What's your mum gonna say to you
Those shoes are really new.

Hey Jo over here
Is it true what I hear
That you put a spider in my shoe?
If you did I'll tell on you.

Charlotte Thorne (10)
St Joseph's RC Primary School, Redhill

Eagle

Soaring high
Up in the sky
Surrounded by blue and white
Way up there
In the fresh air
In full, fast, elegant flight.
Soft and brown
Feathers like down,
And a pair of topaz eyes,
Miles away
He spies his prey,
To feed his young where she lies.
Over hills,
Over mountains,
With the sun-kissed land below
Silver streams
And golden plains
Where rivers rapidly flow.
As the sun
Begins to set
The eagle flies to his nest
Where his young
Are waiting
For their father from the west
To return, with the best.

Bella Turner (10)
St Joseph's RC Primary School, Redhill

Football

As the game starts I feel relaxed
As the game progresses I feel excited
As I receive the ball I feel energetic
When the final whistle blows.
I am elated
We've won!

Aaron O'Callaghan (10)
St Joseph's RC Primary School, Redhill

Noah

N oah my brother
O nly a little boisterous
A lways asking questions
H arder than impossible to answer

S ometimes a bit annoying
T hen sometimes my best friend
J oking, jolly
O ff his head!
H elping me when I am hurt
N icest brother on Earth.

M ind like a monkey, climbing sofas
O bviously mad
O bviously my brother
R ich in humour
E verybody loves him

S mells like chocolaty shampoo
M um's baby boy
I mpossible, irritating, irresistible
T otally in love with his trucks
H appy, he is my brother.

Joshua Moore Smith (10)
St Joseph's RC Primary School, Redhill

Angels

A tiny little angel will protect you from things that may come bad
N o one can stop it from doing its job, what it does best in life
G uarding you all night and guarding you all day
E very time a bell rings an angel gets its wings
L onely or lost it is sure to be there for you
S o do not feel sad or lonely it's always there
beside you, doing its job from God.

Laura Riddell (10)
St Joseph's RC Primary School, Redhill

Seasons

W inter is a time of celebration
I n winter Jesus was born
N ever should we forget him
T ruly a saviour was he
E very year we think of him
R emember all that he has done.

S pring is when new things are born
P laying and dancing for the first ever time
R unning along the new green fields
I n spring all new things grow up
N ever to be small again
G rowing, spreading, happy to be alive.

S ummer is the time for barbecues
U tterly, tasty, Sunday roast
M emorable Bolognaise dishes
M unchy meatball meals
E verlasting scrumptious tastes
R ich chocolate pudding

A utumn is a time of change
U nfolding leaves are no more
T hings start to wither and wilt
U mbrellas blow in this windy season
M atches are lit, fires are born,
N ight rolls in and heaters are on.

Devon Bunyan (10)
St Joseph's RC Primary School, Redhill

I'd Like To Be

I'd like to be a butterfly and fly above the trees
Or maybe be a shimmering fish and swim the seven seas.
What about a little dog, but think of all those fleas?
So just for now I think I'll stick with simply being me!

Jessica Leach (9)
St Joseph's RC Primary School, Redhill

The Bumblebee

I am a little baby bumblebee,
I eat people's lunch and their tea,
No other insect can buzz better than me -
A little baby bumblebee.
I collect pollen to make honey,
I may sting a child or even his mummy,
It could be on the leg or on the knee,
'Cause I'm a little baby bumblebee.

Thomas Li (10)
St Joseph's RC Primary School, Redhill

Bugs

Bugs are anywhere
Any weather they don't care
Any apple, any pear
All they need is good fresh air
Bugs live anywhere
Under the table here and there
Don't worry they'll be there.

Olivia Davies (9)
St Joseph's RC Primary School, Redhill

Love Poem

Love is when my heart feels strong
My stomach hurts
But there's nothing wrong.

I have feelings for you
I know you'll say *No!*
But do you love me too?

There's only one more thing to say and it is true
I don't know how to say this
But I love you!

Fifi Endrojono-Ellis (9)
St Margaret's At Troy Town CE Primary School, Rochester

The Children's Prison

There ahead our prison bars
Past them are endless cars.

Sitting in the bare playground
Nothing fun to be found.

Ushered inside by straight-faced teachers
They look like the devil's creatures.

We are told to read
Why couldn't we be freed.

Maths goes on and on
When will we need this stuff, come on.

English is write that and this
When it is over it is bliss.

Lunch is no happy affair
Two mouthfuls and the plate is bare.

As for the afternoon
We wish it would end so soon

Art is make this line straight
Do they try to frustrate?

PE is last but worst
Get shouted at if you're not first.

At last the day is over and done
Let's go home and have some fun.

We walk away from the bars
And finally join the endless cars.

But the place has left its mark
In the form of hard homework.

So at home when finally at ease
Mum looks up and says, 'What are these?'

And sitting in her right hand there
The dreaded homework boxes bare.

So sitting at the polished table
She says, 'You should be able.'

At last all work is finished
Your brain beaten and diminished.

You lay down your brain
Knowing tomorrow it will begin again.

Liam Dooley (10)
St Margaret's At Troy Town CE Primary School, Rochester

Seasons

Autumn
Crunchy leaves, red, brown
On the grass, hear them rustle
At the park, near town.

Winter
Building a snowman
Just outside in the deep snow
I won't need a fan.

Spring
Easter bunny near
He's bringing eggs, so don't fear
Tomorrow he's here.

Summer
I'm at the seaside
I can see a carnival
I'll go on a ride.

Augusta Cook-Overy (11)
St Margaret's At Troy Town CE Primary School, Rochester

The Bedtime Monster

As I walk to bed each night I tiptoe, tiptoe
Up the stairs in fright.
As I get nearer all I can hear is the cry of
Creaking floorboards.

As I reach the top of the stairs
I stand ready to go in
But do I dare?
I turn the handle
And in the middle a lighted candle.
Like a vandal I ran like the wind.
And there I hid.

I jumped on my bed
With laughter in my head
I curled up in my bed
And there I lay still.

Then I hear a thumping
And a sort of clumping
Coming from under my bed
Then I saw a head
I closed my eyes and went to sleep
And in the morning I found my ted.

Rosemary Acton (10)
St Margaret's At Troy Town CE Primary School, Rochester

The Rat Rap

We live in the sewers
We're great great chewers
Poison's put down
And then we drown.

We're fat and we're lumpy
We're big and we're grumpy.

Some say we're hairy
But we're really scary
We are very cool
The rat gang rule.

We're fat and we're lumpy
We're big and we're grumpy.

We're really skanky
And we are manky
We don't like dogs
And we really hate frogs.

We're fat and we're lumpy
We're big and we're grumpy.

Now our time is over
We're going to sleep in clover
We're going to see our brothers
And all the others.

We're fat and we're lumpy
We're big and we're grumpy.

Olivia McGregor & Chantal Isaac (10)
St Margaret's At Troy Town CE Primary School, Rochester

The Monkey Song

Neither whiskers nor feathers have I
But I have a long tail
And I can
Swing, swing, swing!

Neither a bow nor arrows have I
But I have sharp little teeth
And I can
Swing, swing, swing!

Neither swim nor fly can I
But I can climb tall trees
And I can
Swing, swing, swing!

I master every movement
For I hunt, eat and climb
And I can
Swing, swing, swing!

Jack Cavanagh (10)
St Margaret's At Troy Town CE Primary School, Rochester

Crow Kennings

Feather picker
Grass kicker

Insect meeter
Mountain steeper

High racer
Wind chaser

Small feet
Doesn't eat meat

Seed eater
Jolly beater.

Benjamin Brothwell (10)
St Margaret's At Troy Town CE Primary School, Rochester

The Tiger Song

Neither scales nor feathers have I
But I have a tail, teeth and ears
And *I kill, kill, kill.*

Neither guns nor missiles have I
But I can run fast
And I can
Kill, kill, kill.

Neither radar nor two legs have I
But I have long sharp teeth
And I can
Kill, kill, kill.

Neither arms nor hair have I
But I am the king of the jungle
And I can
Kill, kill, kill.

Jake Gurney (9) & Jack Yerrall (10)
St Margaret's At Troy Town CE Primary School, Rochester

T-Rex

Prehistoric stalker
Amazing walker

Powerful jaws
Threatening claws

Carcass tearer
Animal scarer

Dangerous carnivore
Menacing predator

Balancing well
Never fell

Now read the text
I'm a . . .

Jack Paulley (11)
St Margaret's At Troy Town CE Primary School, Rochester

Snake

I can slither
I love liver

I have no legs
But plenty of eggs

I've got lots of prey
But they never stay

I can live anywhere
Even under the stair

I can strangle
But can't wear a bangle

I can kill
Without a bill

Guess what I am
I'm a snake.

Emma Diprose (10)
St Margaret's At Troy Town CE Primary School, Rochester

Cheetah Kennings

Lightning runner
Jungle stunner

Golden skinned
Black brimmed

Tree climber
Prey stalker

Ripping jaw
Lethal claw

Now who am I
Do you think?

Tommy Boakes (10)
St Margaret's At Troy Town CE Primary School, Rochester

Seasons - Haiku

Autumn
Playing conkers in
The sun is fun, fun, you have
To *win* go and *win*

Winter
Building snowmen is
Fun, they great to build but
They melt in the sun

Spring
Flowers growing and
Blossoms blooming in the spring
They are ev'rywhere

Summer
Getting ready for
Summer eating ice cream on
The beach gone in sea.

Rori Dudley (11)
St Margaret's At Troy Town CE Primary School, Rochester

Tiger Kennings

Very stealthy
Usually healthy

Cattle catcher
Baby snatcher

Massive jaws
Ginormous claws

Meat tearer
Prey scarer

Black knight
Orange bright.

Zachary Lovell (11)
St Margaret's At Troy Town CE Primary School, Rochester

Seasons - Haikus

Autumn
Dead leaves falling from
Trees that are nearly stripped bare
Blown along the ground

Winter
Building snowmen with
Snow that's violently falling
From the cloudless sky

Spring
Sitting on dry wall
Watching flowers blossoming
Enjoying light wind

Summer
Playing on a beach
Soaking in the dazzling sun
Watching shadows skip.

Shu Cheung (11)
St Margaret's At Troy Town CE Primary School, Rochester

Snappy Eater Kennings

Snappy eater
Four-legged creature

Eats meat
Scaly feet

Spiky tail
Fierce male

Dark green
Extremely mean

Swamp dweller
Grumpy feller

I'm an alligator.

Ben Williams (11)
St Margaret's At Troy Town CE Primary School, Rochester

Seasons In Rochester

Summer
Licking ice lollies
At the coast, children playing
At the local park

Spring
Flowers blossoming,
No more rain, just lots of wind
Lambs have come to play

Winter
Sledging down the hills
That's what children do, yes and
Look at all the tracks.

Autumn
Trees are losing leaves
They're falling onto the ground
Conkers everywhere.

Joshua Hancock (10)
St Margaret's At Troy Town CE Primary School, Rochester

Sneaky And Sly

Sneaky and sly
Silent and shy

Tears flood
Its skin is smooth

Sharp claws
Lovely paws

Its sharp teeth
Are very mean

Orange and black
And not very fat

It's a
Tiger

Amber Whiting (11)
St Margaret's At Troy Town CE Primary School, Rochester

Round The Seasons We Go

Autumn
In the cornfield day
Waving at the blowing wind
Carolling all the way

Winter
Let the snow fall down soft
Go to bed my darling town
Go and drift to sleep

Spring
Rainbow spread your wings
While flowers collect their bees
Animals wake up please

Summer
Sea is leaking now
Come to wash your feet quite clean
Push the sand away.

Vabyanti Endrojono-Ellis (10)
St Margaret's At Troy Town CE Primary School, Rochester

Summer Sun

Summer sun
Is lots of fun
When you are on the beach
My skin is tanning like a peach
Summer sun.

When you are swimming in the sea
You feel as light as a bumblebee
Having sand fights with your friends
Hoping the day will never end
Summer sun.

Joshua Howell
St Peter's CE Primary School, Folkestone

Guess What I Am?

Males mating
Mothers hating
Rapid running
Mothers loving

Shoe lace knickers
Little warm pickers
Little egg layers
Big time wasters.

Adam Bartlett (10)
St Peter's CE Primary School, Folkestone

Dreams

Fairies and mermaids and witches and
wizards
Tornadoes and storms and dragons and blizzards
Dreams and lightning fairy tales too
Stories and fluffy clouds just for you
Rough seas and calm seas and lullaby songs
These are the things for which my heart longs.

Beth Gillan (10)
St Peter's CE Primary School, Folkestone

Seasons

See the sea in summer
Eating apples in autumn
All on the beach playing in the sun
Snuggle in bed in the middle of winter
Outside the snow is falling
Nestlings being born in spring
Season's greetings come at Christmas.

Shane Ridley (10)
St Peter's CE Primary School, Folkestone

A Walk In The Forest

I was walking in the forest
When I came across a bear
I asked him to 'move it'
But he didn't care.
He got in a stress over and over again
He got in a stress until half past ten
I called my dad, I called my mum
He looked at them and said, 'Yum, yum, yum.'
My dad started to shout and run about
He looked like a football lout.
He frightened the bear and gave a scare
It scurried away like a startled hare.

Sebastian Weightman (10)
St Peter's CE Primary School, Folkestone

Kittens

Kittens
Cute, fluffy
Walking, growing, jumping
A family friend
Adorable.

Kayleigh Gilson (10)
St Peter's CE Primary School, Folkestone

The Fun Day

I went to the park one day
I wanted to go and play
I had lots of fun
But got burnt by the sun
Now I have nothing to say.

Ellen Gregory (10)
St Peter's CE Primary School, Folkestone

Bumblebee

Bumblebee
Bumblebee
Come and visit me
In my garden of flowers
You'll 'bee' busy for hours.

Bumblebee
Bumblebee
Go back to your hive
And inform all the others
It will be just jive.

Bumblebee
Bumblebee
The queen bee is fat
She is so greedy.

She's as fat as my cat.

Jaryd Lohan (11)
St Peter's CE Primary School, Folkestone

Spiders

Spiders, spiders are so quiet
Spiders, spiders go on a diet
Spiders, spiders like the dust
Spiders, spiders play in the rust.

Spiders, spiders are so scary
Spiders, spiders are so hairy
Spiders, spiders are so sneaky
Spiders, spiders are so cheeky.

Spiders, spiders sometimes leap
Spiders, spiders have a peak
Spiders, spiders are so tiny
Spiders, spiders act so kindly.

Robbie Westbrook (10)
St Peter's CE Primary School, Folkestone

The Earth

The Earth is cool
The Earth is fun
It is my planet
Number one.

It has many people
Some smart, some not
Some have a little
Some have the lot!

Lovely food, different flavour
In the big round Earth.
Lots of lovely tastes to savour
It might increase my girth.

It has two places after death
Light, lovely Heaven and hot Hell
Better be good, better be bad
If you didn't fly up you fell.

The scary demon
Down below the ground
If you are bad
You'll never be found.

Chani Sanger (10)
St Peter's CE Primary School, Folkestone

Holiday In York

We went to a place called York
My sister ate lots of pork
I had lots of fun
Sister ate a ton
And accidentally ate up the fork.

Zoe Chapman (9)
St Peter's CE Primary School, Folkestone

Guess Who! Kennings

Great eater
High leaper
Leg lover
Fast runner
Little insect
Music maker
Leg shaker.

I'm a grasshopper.

Michael Bridges (11)
St Peter's CE Primary School, Folkestone

The Beach

As I sit on the beach
With the smooth and silky sand
I watch the sea roll up and down
As the sand runs through my hand.

As the sun sets and the moon rises
I look out to the ocean sea
I hear the beautiful tune of a whale
I see the splash of a dolphin's tail.

Naomi Nicol (9)
St Peter's CE Primary School, Folkestone

Holiday In Spain

I once went on holiday to Spain
My sister was a pain
It was loads of fun
Got burnt by the sun
Then got back on the plane.

Zoe Perry (10)
St Peter's CE Primary School, Folkestone

Summer And Winter

S ummer sun
U mbrellas away
M elting chocolate
M ums shouting
E njoying fun in the garden
R elaxing in the summer sun

W et and cold
I cy windows
N ice warm cuddles
T ea steaming hot
E ating biscuits
R ains falling from the sky.

Natalie Atherton (11)
St Peter's CE Primary School, Folkestone

Red

Red tastes like hot chilli peppers
Red looks like an erupting volcano
Red smells like bonfire night
Red feels like a tomato
Red sounds like fire engines.

Marcus Williams (11)
St Peter's CE Primary School, Folkestone

Mrs White

Mrs White had a fright
Very late in the night
She saw a ghost eating toast
Whilst balancing on a lamp post.

Bradley Weightman (11)
St Peter's CE Primary School, Folkestone

Springtime Poem

There was a month called May
Where all the lambs went grey
One day the sun said, 'Hey,
Springtime is here today.'
Everyone was full of joy
Especially the boy named Soy,
Because his little sister
Said, 'Go! Go!'

Daisy-May Weightman (9)
St Peter's CE Primary School, Folkestone

Guess What I Am?

Plays at night in its wheel
Stores food in its cheeks
Four legs
Very soft.

Hops
Has a very fluffy tail
Lives in a hole
Very long ears.

Shunna Wallace (9)
St Peter's CE Primary School, Folkestone

Rover

There was a dog from Dover
Whose owners called him Rover
He once chased a cat
Which ended up flat
Then he ended up run over.

Jordan Redworth (9)
St Peter's CE Primary School, Folkestone

What Am I? Kennings

Slow mover
Shell armour
Egg layer
Green colour

        Blood sucker
        Brown colour
        High jumper
        Skin irritator.

Jaye Mynard (11)
St Peter's CE Primary School, Folkestone

Josh

There once was a boy called Josh
Who thought he was terribly posh
He had plenty of money
And thought that was funny
This is the story of Josh.

Jake Gregson (10)
St Peter's CE Primary School, Folkestone

The Fish

There once was a fish who had a very bad tummy
The others thought it was funny
He thought it was sad
He thought it was very bad
So he was a very bad lad.

Caroline Wiechmann (7)
St Peter's CE Primary School, Folkestone

Blue

Blue looks like the glittering sea
in the summer,
Blue tastes like fish and chips
in last night's paper,
Blue smells like the salty sea
in stormy weather,
Blue sounds like the crashing of
waves on a seaweed covered rock,
Blue feels like the smooth, white sails
on a boat.

Gabriella Dawkes (11)
St Peter's CE Primary School, Folkestone

Red

Red is fire burning in Hell!
Red is hate getting so angry!
Red is volcano's erupting, killing
everything in its path!
Red is blood running down the skin!
Red is death . . . no one left.

Elliot Langston (10)
St Peter's CE Primary School, Folkestone

Red Berries Red

Where are you?
Your bright red berries
Shining through
In the garden proud you stand
All against dying land.

Marcus Palmer (11)
St Peter's CE Primary School, Folkestone

The Dragon Named Dave

There once was a dragon named Dave
Who loved his shiny golden cave
He had a spiky green tail that always failed,
He was never never brave.

Albert Gregson (9)
St Peter's CE Primary School, Folkestone

The Lazy Dragon

Once there was a dragon
Who thought he'd get a lift on a wagon.
He was too lazy to fly
'All that energy would make me high,'
He said as the wagon rolled by.

Simon Gillan (8)
St Peter's CE Primary School, Folkestone

The Fish

There was a fish called Leigh
Who swam all the sea
When he got there he was sad
And he thought it was bad
And he wished he was free.

Leigh Chapman (8)
St Peter's CE Primary School, Folkestone

The Brave Dragon Dave

There once was a dragon named Dave
The people thought he was brave
He breathed lots of fire
His breath smelt dire
So he went and hid in his cave.

Damon Greenway (8)
St Peter's CE Primary School, Folkestone

Never, Never, Never

Never, never, never do that Louis
Never, never, never eat that chewy
Never, never, never do that Ellie
Never, never, never eat that jelly
Never, never, never do that Ryan
Never, never, never eat that iron
Never, never, never do that Brooke
Never, never, never eat that book
Never, never, never do that Katie
Never, never, never eat our matie
Never, never, never do that pickle
Never, never, never eat that nickle
Never, never, never do that Tom
Never, never, never eat that song
Never, never, never do that Elle
Never, never, never eat that well.

Ellie Hardinges & Louis Milioto (7)
Sedley's CE Primary School, Southfleet

Hands Up, Hands Down

Hands up, hands down.
Make a smile, make a frown.
Yellow class is the best,
Even though we do lots of tests!
In maths we do quick quiz,
Some of the children have to mind
their own bizz!
Music is as fun as can be,
Our teacher always drinks a cup of
tea!
In assembly we sing a song,
While the church bell goes
Bing bong!

Philippa Coppitters (8)
Sedley's CE Primary School, Southfleet

What's In The Drawer

What's in the drawer?
What's in the drawer?
If it's sweets
I want more,
Or is it an
Axe to chop off our heads?
Or a secret weapon to tear us to shreds?
Or maybe it's just . . .
> Homework!

George Summerfield (9)
Sedley's CE Primary School, Southfleet

Pow-Wow Point Lodge

Pow-wow point lodge is a beautiful place,
People say it's full of peace and full of grace,
It's a place full of wonderfulness and a place full of dreams.
But I've got to see it in my own two eyes to see what it means.

Annabel Coppitters (9)
Sedley's CE Primary School, Southfleet

Shop, Shop, Shopping

When my mummy goes shopping
There is no stop, stop, stopping in the market.
When we go in the car
There's no stop, stop, stopping
With the shop, shop, shopping.

Ellie-Rose Thomas (7) & Chelsie Fuller (8)
Sedley's CE Primary School, Southfleet

World War Two

W orld War Two was dangerous
O h why did it have to happen?
R uined streets and towns
L oads of people fought
D isasters happened

W ar was dangerous
A ngry Hitler was too
R uined streets and towns

T rains left full of children
W ar was a disaster
O h it was sad.

Hannah Mitchell (8)
Sedley's CE Primary School, Southfleet

The Circus School

Oh damn! I've dropped my thud ball
I tried to play it cool
But Mr Bungo heard the noise
And pinned me to the wall.

'You stupid boy,' he growled at me
His red nose pressed to mine,
His eyebrows twitched, he curled his lip
His breath, it smelt of wine.

Her sent me to the ringmaster's room
For six strokes of the best
He pulled out his smooth shiny black whip
And hit me on the chest.

Oh no it's time for boring lunch
It's custard pies again
We have the same every day
I'd rather eat a roasted hen.

Daisy Cropper (10) & Alex Hyder (11)
Sellindge County Primary School, Ashford

Humpty Dumpty Drank Too Much

Humpty Dumpty sat in a pub
Drinking vodka and Coke
He liked to have a lot to drink
Although it always made him stink
He was rather a joke.

It started when he was at school
The bullyling and names
'Here comes Humpty round and chubby
A big fat egg look at Tubby
You can't play in our game.'

'You're too fat to sit on a chair
You just keep rolling off'
At first he took it on the chin
But then he started to drink gin
Then later switched to Smirnoff.

As Humpty Dumpty got older
His drinking did get worse
All day he would stay in the pub
Guzzling vodka by the tub
His boozing was a curse.

Ryan Martin (10)
Sellindge County Primary School, Ashford

I Am The Magnificent Magical Elephant

I don't eat peanuts or leaves
I scoff mice and rats
I don't drink water
I slurp pink wine
I don't carry logs
I lift school buildings.

Matthew Pryce (7)
Sellindge County Primary School, Ashford

Me And My Annoying Friend

She started it
She pulled my hair
She went mad like she was having a fit
And she took my ball and threw it in the air.

She pushed me in the line
She kicked me under the table
She hurt my spine
She ripped the legs off the tables.

Then that was it! You came and said,
'Stop it now, it's home time.'
'Can we go now?'

Demi Williams (11)
Sellindge County Primary School, Ashford

I Am The Excellent Pony

I don't eat grass or pony nuts
I scoff mountain tops and clay
I don't drink water or creamy milk
I slurp lava and ink
I don't canter in any normal way
I fly as fast as an eagle
I don't neigh normally
I screech so loud I could deafen somebody
I don't sleep on the grass
I sleep on the moon or sometimes trees.

Emily Hare (9)
Sellindge County Primary School, Ashford

The Thud Ball

I am
a
juggling
ball and
sometimes get
hit on the
wall. Mostly
I get hit on the
floor, but when
people practice
I get hit
even more.

Liam Bishopp (9)
Sellindge County Primary School, Ashford

The Whizzing Dog

I am a whizzing dog
I eat electricity or fire and nuts
I don't eat biscuits or meat
I don't drink water or milk
I drink diesel and red wine or beer
I don't sleep in a basket or on a pillow
I sleep in a bed or on a cloud
I don't chase cats or birds
I chase insects and bite flies.

Rionne Tucker
Sellindge County Primary School, Ashford

Juggling!

Juggle the balls in
the air
Try to catch them
here and there.

                I'll help you do
                a trick or two
                Then I'll leave it
                up to you.

Try to do it in
front of a crowd
Don't be nervous
be proud!

Billy Cross
Sellindge County Primary School, Ashford

An Amazing Magical Frog

I am the magical frog
I don't eat flies
I scoff bugs
I don't drink milk
I drink water
I don't sleep on the lily leaves
I sleep underwater
I don't chase birds
I chase fleas.

Joseph Beaney (8)
Sellindge County Primary School, Ashford

The Circus School

I've dropped my ball on the floor!
Will Smiller notice? (Miserable bore!)
If he does he'll whack my bun
A circus school should be fun.

My stick went through the window! Smash!
I'll be whipped badly by Slash.
I hit Ian our teacher, with my Chinese ribbons
He threw me in, with his bad gibbons.

I dropped one of my wooden stilts
And hit a clown wearing kilts
I swung around my favourite pois
The pois went through and hit some boys.

Us boys are clever we tell lies
So we don't eat those custard pies
They make us feel very sick
Especially when they're really thick.

I'm going to assembly to get my face
I'd better get on at a faster pace
I hope it looks really nice
Cos somebody's looks like mice.

Ronny Shorter (11)
Sellindge County Primary School, Ashford

Stilts

I'm on
Stilts
And
I'm
Very
Tall

I'm on
Stilts
And
I will
Not
Fall.

James Ashman
Sellindge County Primary School, Ashford

Explain Yourself

He pulled my nose
I kicked his shin
He said he would tell his sister Zoe
I said I would win.

>I held his leg
>He pinched my skin
>I said I would make him beg
>He said he would get his mate Tim.

He shouted and swore
I said I would get Mum on him
He said you are made to come back for more
I pulled his nose in front of him.

>I called for Dad
>He said shut up
>I shouted you're mad
>He said Mum will hit the top.

And then Mum you came
It was only over a tower!
Can we go now
We've been standing here one hour?

Jack Stephens (11)
Sellindge County Primary School, Ashford

Stilts

Stilts
look
fun
but
you
have
to be
clever!

One
second's
rest
and
whoops
you're
in the
heather.

Bryony Homewood
Sellindge County Primary School, Ashford

The Magic Fly Frog

I am a magic fly frog
I don't eat flies
I don't eat grubs
I eat frogs
I eat mixed fried frog
I am a flying frog
I am not a frog that jumps
I am a frog that tries to fly
I am a frog that always gets fried
I am not a frog that lives in a pond
I live in a lady's sink
I don't chase flies
I chase fingers.

Chelsea Williams
Sellindge County Primary School, Ashford

I Am The Daring Dragon

I don't eat fried soldiers or a brave knight
I eat a princess in my sight
I don't guard a castle on a volcano
I guard a castle in a tornado
I don't fry boulders or a grave at night
I fry toast with all my might
I don't sleep around the castle
I sleep around a French parcel.

Jed Deal
Sellindge County Primary School, Ashford

Hard Life At Circus School

Life is hard at circus school
All we do is juggle balls
Look! Hear comes the Ringmaster
We had better work faster.

It's a hard life at circus school
All we do is play the fool
We girls don't get on with the boys
Because they always nick our bow ties.

My Daisy-Sprayer is boring now
Although everyone says wow
Sometimes my friends laugh at my jokes
When they don't I give them a soak.

At playtime we work hard
Although we work in the yard
I always thought life would be fun at circus
But I've changed my mind.

At lunch we always have custard pies
Everyone says I hope we survive,
The dinner lady laughs at us
When a custard pie comes flying at us.

Shannon Houghton (11)
Sellindge County Primary School, Ashford

Feathery Feather

A circus came to our school
They made me laugh
And I hit my head on the wall.
I loved the acrobats
They tickled me with the
feathery feathers
I snapped the feathers
with my leathers.

Amber Bull (7)
Sellindge County Primary School, Ashford

Tell Me What Happened

She hit me
So I slapped her face
She kicked my shin
So I trod on her lace.

She pushed me down
And sat on my head
She trod on my foot
And I said she was dead!

She pulled my hair
I stamped on her hairband
She spat at my face
I pinched her hand.

She bit my arm
And that's when you came
But we're friends now
It . . . it was only a game.

Lauren Burgess (11)
Sellindge County Primary School, Ashford

The Plate

Start to spin it
Look at the base
Try and balance it
Off your face!
Start to spin it
Try to win
Do not drop it
Or sit on a pin!

Lewis Coates (9)
Sellindge County Primary School, Ashford

The Whirling Hamster

I am the whirring hapster
I don't eat nuts or biscuits
I chew wood, insects
And comics
I don't drink water or milk
I slurp lava, vinegar and dog saliva
I don't sleep in a cage
I snooze on the moon
And on the stars too.
I don't chase flies
I chase shooting stars
And teachers.

Emel Larsen (8)
Sellindge County Primary School, Ashford

The Juggling Balls

Funny
Bouncy
Flying
Juggly

Smooth
Fun
Colourful
Round

Noisy
Spinning
Thuddy
Flippy
Balls.

Megan Bishop
Sellindge County Primary School, Ashford

The Circus School

Oh thud! I dropped my balls!
'Oi,' the ringmaster calls
Pick em up quick, or you'll get the whip
Oh thud! I dropped my balls.

We're sick of custard pies
Pink ones, yellow ones
All straight in your eyes!
We're sick of custard pies!

Here comes the ringmaster
He's holding the Black Whip book
We shiver and our legs shake faster
Here comes the ringmaster!

Pedal go, pedal go, goes too fast,
I wish, I wish I could skip this class
When I get on I fall straight off
Pedal, go pedal go, goes too fast!

Yes it's playtime, I can read a book
People still in lesson, try to take a look.
I learned my tables, I added and took
Yes it's playtime, I can read a book!

It's the last day of the term, the day I get my face,
Will it be cool for a complete disgrace?
It's a race to get the best face!
Today's the last of term!

Ashleigh Williamson (11)
Sellindge County Primary School, Ashford

The Chinese Ribbons

These are Chinese ribbons
They are colourful and nice
They can fall on the ground
And launch in the sky
They can twist and turn.

Shelby Kennett
Sellindge County Primary School, Ashford

Humpty Dumpty

Humpty Dumpty sat in a pub
Drinking vodka and Coke
He liked to have a lot to drink
Though it made him stink
He was rather a joke.

It started when he was at school
The bullying and names
'Here comes Humpty round and chubby
A big fat egg look at tubby
You can't play in our games.'

You're too fat to sit on a chair
You just keep rolling off'
At first he took it on the chin
But then he started to drink gin
Then later switched to Smirnoff.

He kept wanting more and more
He could not stop
And then he drank and drank
And then his eyes sank
He could not sit without a plop.

He staggered onto the floor
He retched and retched
All the time he vomited
He went off to sleep
Later he woke up never to repeat.

Abdul Ahad (10)
Sellindge County Primary School, Ashford

The Chinese Ribbons

These are the Chinese ribbons
They are colourful and pretty
You can twist and turn them
They are all different shapes.

Kerrie Alexander (9)
Sellindge County Primary School, Ashford

The Magical Unicorn

I am the magical unicorn
I don't eat hay or straw
I scoff fish and meat
I don't drink milk or red wine
I slurp water and electricity.
I don't sleep in a stable
Or in a house
I doze on a bed.
I don't chase birds
Or mice or people.
I chase penguins and smelly pigs.

Shanon King
Sellindge County Primary School, Ashford

The Magical Horse

I am a magical horse
I don't eat grass or hay
I graze dung and mouldy sausages
I don't chase other horses
I do scare mice and birds
I don't slurp water
I drink vinegar and white wine
Mixed together
I don't doze in a stable
I sleep in a cage.

Lauren Hyder (8)
Sellindge County Primary School, Ashford

The Happy Horse

I am the happy horse
I don't run round the fields all day
I skip and jump and mostly play.

When it comes to mealtimes I eat
Lots of food and a yummy treat.

Also when it's time to drink
I have some water, don't you think.

I also sleep somewhere nice,
On a bit of grass next to some mice.

I sometimes play with my friends all day
But when I'm tired I have some hay.

Sharon Fuller (9)
Sellindge County Primary School, Ashford

The Fantastic Dog

I am the fantastic dog
I do not eat meat or biscuits
I scoff monkeys, butterflies and grass
I love everyone
I don't like water
I slurp blood, milk and petrol
I don't sleep in a dog's bed
I lay on my owner's bed and settee.

Kerrie Alexander (9)
Sellindge County Primary School, Ashford

The Circus School

Mr Coco drives me loco
Teaching me the thudding balls
I can't help it, I can't catch them
And the diabolo always falls.

We are waiting in the hall
For the Whip Book to be read
The Whip Book is as black as coal
And the writing is blood-red.

Then we went to the dinner hall
Grabbed my plate, grabbed my food
Splat, threw a pie in Coco's face
Got shouted at for being rude.

Got the 'six of the best' again
I stood by the circus tent.
The Ringmaster said, 'Don't do it again.'
That teacher is surely bent.

We're in the leaver's assembly
I am now going to get my face
Now I am a proper clown
Whoopee! It's time to pack my case.

Nishat Rashid (10) & Suzanne Curtis (11)
Sellindge County Primary School, Ashford

I Am The Magical Tiger

I don't eat meat and fish
I scoff magical mice and cheese
I don't drink milk or water
I slurp magical red wine and vinegar
I don't sleep in a cave
I do doze in a tunnel
I don't chase birds or rabbits
I do chase deer and lightning.

Bethany Old (7)
Sellindge County Primary School, Ashford

The Feather

Billy had a feather
It came down to the Earth
Or so he thought.

Billy had a feather
It came from the skies
Or so he thought.

Billy had a feather
It came from the clouds
Or so he thought.

Billy had a feather
It came from the heavens
Or so he thought.

Billy had a feather
It came from an angel
And he was right.

Joshua Walton (10)
Sellindge County Primary School, Ashford

I Am A Magical Dragon

I don't eat people and animals
I eat gold and silver and diamonds
I don't drink blood and oil
I drink lager and Coca-Cola.
I don't sleep in a castle or on people
I sleep on a magic cloud or lava.
I don't chase people or dragons
I chase warriors and kinds.

Joe Williams
Sellindge County Primary School, Ashford

On The Circus School

I have dropped a thudding ball!
Will I ever be an A+ Fool?
Wally the clown will give me a kick
And shout at me till I feel sick
Why can't I catch the thudding ball?

Now we learn the Diabolo
But how to do I do not know
Piggo the clown will not like me
If I can't do it he'll smack my knee
Now why can't we not do Diabolo?

Now it's time for lunch
We now start to munch
Ningo's crummy custard pies
We have them every day, that's no surprise
I've had enough of custard pies.

The Ringmaster is here
Teachers and pupils clap and cheer
It's graduation day at last
I'll get my *face!* I have passed!
It's goodbye Circus School.

Roanna Williams (11)
Sellindge County Primary School, Ashford

I Am The Magical Dog

I don't eat meat or chews
I don't drink water or milk
I scoff thunder or vinegar
I drink oil or red blood
I sleep in the bin.

Yasmin Shorter (8)
Sellindge County Primary School, Ashford

Well What Happened?

He lifted his fist
So I called him names
Then he said,
'Stop playing a game.'

                        He glared at me
                        And I didn't like that
                        So I punched him and
                        Said, 'You are fat.'

My dad always said
That I should fight back,
So I kicked him in the ribs
And we heard a crack.

                        I started to cry
                        Really, really bad
                        I was very angry
                        And I felt kind of sad.

I shouted for a nurse
As he tried to stand up
Then we heard a howl
I said, 'It's only a pup.'

                        The dog came in view
                        And it started to bite me
                        We heard someone shout,
                        'Come back here Dee!'

That's when you came Miss
You shooed the dog away
But we're friends now aren't we
We've stood here all play.

Liam Bailey (11)
Sellindge County Primary School, Ashford

At Playtime

He nodded his head
So I nodded mine
I said he wet the bed
He said, 'You little swine.'

        He punched me in the nose
        So I started to cry
        Then his voice rose
        I didn't know why.

He pulled my hair
So I punched him in the lip
His eyes started to flair
And I felt like a pip.

        My dad always said
        I should walk away
        But this time
        I am going to stay.

I wanted a nurse
And I started to cry
But then it got worse
I thought I was going to die.

        I said my big sister
        Would give him a whack
        He said his brother
        Would give me a smack.

And that's when you came Miss
And pulled us apart
But we're friends now aren't we?
We didn't mean to start.

George Tanner (11)
Sellindge County Primary School, Ashford

The Argument

I raised my foot
He raised his hand
I said leave off
He pushed me in the sand.

        He grabbed my head,
        I got really mad
        He said to me,
        'I'll sort you out lad.'

He kicked my leg
I said to him,
'You're silly to do that
And you're so dim.'

        So I said to him,
        'You shouldn't say that
        Because it is rude
        You smelly old bat.'

Then I saw the head
Standing in the background
So I said to Jim,
'Do not make a sound.'

        But I couldn't hear him
        And I was fed up
        So I shouted out loudly
        And the head dropped his cup.

Then you came Sir
And grabbed us by our ears
Then shouted at us loudly
So we are almost in tears.

Katherine Pryce (10)
Sellindge County Primary School, Ashford

Two Little Dicky Birds

In England it was very chilly
The birds flew south, they aren't silly
Across the ocean deep and blue
Peter and Paul flew and flew.

Looking for a place to stay
They saw some huts made of clay
Down they swooped to the ground
Amongst the feet of the people brown.

They sipped some water, ate some grain
In case it would not ever rain
They hired a very small old house
Which contained a merry old mouse.

They slept in the hut, and found a nut
Got a knife and used it to cut
They made up a very bad lie
They were seen so they started to fly.

When they were in England it was warmer than before
So they pecked at a worm on an apple core.
They flew over to their old nest
And said 'Snug as a bug is best.'

Alexander Yardy (10)
Sellindge County Primary School, Ashford

My Manky Monkey

My manky monkey is as manky as mouldy fruit
And is as strong as a super-strong wrestler.
It is as fierce as a school bully stealing dinner money
And as noisy as a guard dog attacking a burglar!
It is as scary as a dark night on Hallowe'en
And is as famous as the famous queen.
It can dance, it can jive and ha it is mine!

Sam Baker (11)
Sellindge County Primary School, Ashford

The Scarves

He threw them high
right up to the sky

What a marvellous sight
when he caught them with
all his might

He threw them again
and boy, that was
impressive!

Harry Stephens (8)
Sellindge County Primary School, Ashford

Dancing

Dancing is the best
Better than all the rest
Latin and ballroom
Is my thing
It just makes me
Want to get up and swing.
The jive and the cha cha
Are my favourite
I love them both
What about you?
So if you want to feel alive
Then go to school and learn to jive
And you could become
The king of rock and roll
So don't sit and watch TV
Come and dance, just like me!

Liberty Francis (10)
Shernold School, Maidstone

My Football Match

I wake up in the morning
And wonder what day it is today?
Stretching and yawning
Hooray - it's Saturday!

We're playing for the junior cup
I see the time, I must get up.
I have a wash and find my gear
Get myself dressed, Mum shouts 'Hurry up dear.'

I arrive at the match, it's time to begin
The whistle blows, I hope that we win.
I'm playing up front, running up and down
We're called Blue Eagles, they're a team in our town.

The ball comes towards me and I take a shot,
Will it go in, oh dear, I think not.
Jimmy's our goalie, he's not very good
He swings on the bar, I don't think he should.

He's let in another, that makes it six-nil
I still hope we win, but I don't think we will.
The whistle blows, the end of the game
We've lost the match, we know who's to blame!

At the end of the match I hand back my shirt
I'm battered and bruised and covered in dirt.
I try to keep smiling, I'm tired and weak,
But I'm not going to worry, there's always next week!

Jamie Thresher (8)
Shernold School, Maidstone

I Look In The Mirror

I look in the mirror and who do I see
I see no one looking back at me
I've faded away just disappeared, that is what I've always feared
No one noticed me except my friends
And now they're gone, my life must end.

Rhea Tanna (9)
Shernold School, Maidstone

Summer Days!

Summer days are the best
At the pool
On the beach
On a cruise
Beside the sea
Making sandcastles
That's where I want to be.

Summer days are the best
Where flowers bloom
Trees begin to have leaves
Butterflies come out
Fresh strawberries
Fresh cherries
That's what I like about summer.

Methula Nanthakumasan (10)
Shernold School, Maidstone

If I Could Drive

If I could drive
I would try to survive
I'll be as quick as a flash
But avoid a crash
I could go anywhere I want
A bar, a club or a restaurant.

It's just no fun
When you are young
Because you can't drive!
So when I'm older I'll
     drive alive!

Bethany Gerrish (10)
Shernold School, Maidstone

Canoeing

Floating in a boat in summer
Is just what I like to do
Gently paddling down the river
In my sky blue canoe.

I see the cars in the field
And the ponies on the hill
I see the reeds and the bulrushes
As I float past the windmill.

I listen to the gulls calling
And the windmill sails turning
I hear the ducks a bobbing
And the ducklings busy learning how to swim.

It is so peaceful on my boat
That I feel as if I could sleep
Forever, forever
I feel as if I could sleep, forever.

Ben Harvey (9)
Shernold School, Maidstone

Let Us Go

Let us go,
You and I,
To where the silver oceans lie.
Let us go you and me
To the deepest depths of the sea
For there and only there
We can be free,
Together, just you and me.
Best friends forever, you and me.

Nancy Watts (10)
Shernold School, Maidstone

Teacher's Pet

There he goes, the teacher's pet
In the test, what will he get?
Let me guess . . . straight A's
In the library, he spends most of his days.

Glasses balanced on his nose
His shoelaces done in neat little bows
He never has a hair out of place
Nor a speck of dirt on his clean shining face.

He gives his teacher an apple a day
'Here you go teacher,' he always will say
So there you have it, the teacher's pet
The slimiest boy you ever have met.

Alexandra Browne (11)
Shernold School, Maidstone

The Other World

I look into a mirror, I see another world,
Wait, there's no other world so it must be my twin,
But I don't have a twin.
This is starting to annoy me now, especially the copying.
Great, it's mouthing my words,
Luckily it can't speak,
And the room is the same as mine,
So it must be another world,
No, but how can it?
Right, I've had enough of this, I'm going.

Christabel Webb (9)
Shernold School, Maidstone

Medieval War

Our weapons are ready, we're off to war,
We shall kill the poor.
We are the Scottish
And the hottest
Where's the blood
Like a river in the mud
We have peace,
Our peace will never cease!

Hamish Massie (7)
Shernold School, Maidstone

Euro 2004 Portugal

The football is about to start
I can't wait to stay up late
To watch England they are great
David Beckham will be brill
For crossing balls to give a thrill
I hope we win the Euro cup but if we don't
We will never give up!

Tom Cosgrove (9)
Shernold School, Maidstone

Daisy And Lay Lay

Daisy and Lay Lay are my favourite things,
Running, jumping in the rings.
They are horses you see,
I like to ride on Daisy's back with Lay Lay beside.
They trot and canter on the grass
Time with them I like to pass.

Alice Jepheart (8)
Shernold School, Maidstone

The Rainforest

Monkeys swinging from tree to tree
Oh what a life it would be
Eating and swinging all day long
That's a monkey to me.

Frogs jumping out of the water
Eating flies with their very long tongues
Camouflage like a leaf or maybe a tree
That's a frog to me.

Snakes so thin and long
Killing its prey one by one
Hissing and eating all day long
There are so many snakes to me,
Can't you see.

George Edwardes (11)
Shernold School, Maidstone

What I Find In My Desk

A ripe peach with an ugly bruise
A pair of stinky tennis shoes
A day-old ham and cheese on rye
A swimsuit that I left to dry
A pencil that glows in the dark
Some bubblegum found in the park
A paper bag with cookie crumbs
An old letter by a stupid bully saying 'You're so dumb'
A spelling test I almost failed
A letter that I should have mailed
And one more thing I must confess
A note from the teacher: *clean up this mess!*

Edward Craddock (10)
Shernold School, Maidstone

Puppies And Kittens

Puppies and kittens, I love them so much
They're nice to stroke and nice to touch.

I love puppies, they're the best,
They never want to have a rest.

My kitten loves to be surprised
But when she is hungry, she starts to cry.

Some people don't like puppies, because they growl,
Some people don't like kittens because they howl.

All the animals in the world I love so much
Especially those I like to touch.

Ami-Kay Gordon (8)
Shernold School, Maidstone

Summer

The sun is out
Without a doubt
Flowers are bright
What a wonderful sight
Butterflies are hatching
While waves are catching
The sky is clear
While Dad's drinking beer
Go to the beach
And have a peach.

Anna Davis (9)
Shernold School, Maidstone

Dinosaurs

Dinosaurs, dinosaurs,
Herbivores and carnivores,
All as good as can be
Everybody likes them
Just don't entice them
Or they could make you
Dead meat!

But nothing is as interesting
As a dinosaur's remaining thing,
Filled with amazing facts
Oh everybody likes them
But they can be a little frightsome!
So I suppose that's that.

So now comes the end
Of the dinosaur's reign
Some say an explosion came
Oh I still miss them
I wish they were still here today.

Pranav Kasetti (9)
Shernold School, Maidstone

Summer

Delicious, yummy, tasty ice creams
Cold, runny, freezing smoothies
Juicy, marvellous red strawberries.

Pretty, lovely, colourful T-shirts
Cute, smart, long dresses
Shady, protective, fabulous sunglasses.

Warm, hot, slippery swimming pool
Wavy, salty sandy beach
Smooth, sensitive, moisturising suncream.

Shelby-Jo Bellamy (10)
Shernold School, Maidstone

Summer

Summer brings flowers
And glorious hours
A bright gold sun
And lots of fun
Wake up next day
Happy and gay
Run outside and play!

Summer is more fun
Than any other time
It is simply divine
Summer brings baby dogs and frogs
Bats and cats,
And things like that,
I *do* love summer!

Joanna Harvey (7)
Shernold School, Maidstone

The Summer Poem

The sun is out in the day, the moon out at night,
The sun is yellow, the moon is white
And the toad crossed the road at night,
With one big smile and one big grin,
Saw the pond and jumped right in.

The birds are out in the day, the badgers are out at night,
The birds are brown, the badgers are black and white,
The birds fly high in the sky, the badgers crawl on the ground.

Charlotte May (10)
Shernold School, Maidstone

School

School can be boring
School can be fun
It provides lots of knowledge
For everyone.

Bell goes at nine
All queue up
Into our classrooms
We all trot.

Maths, English, science
With a break in-between
History, geography
Then lunch in the canteen.

The afternoon is better
With drama and PE
Very quickly
We're off home having tea.

But it doesn't end there,
There's still more to do!
A little bit of homework
Then a game or two.

Michaela Savage (11)
Shernold School, Maidstone

My Cat Ami

My cat Ami's whiskers stick out
She twitches them as she walks about
She wags her tail as she walks
She goes out and she stalks
She never comes back in
She only comes when we rattle her tin.

Abbie Prentice (8)
Shernold School, Maidstone

Martin And Sophia

I love my cousins very much,
They mean the world to me.
No one could ever replace them,
They're as loving as can be.

They're active fun and playful,
Sometimes I can't keep up.
They will play with me all day long,
Until I've had enough.

But then again I don't mind,
As long as they are here.
So I can love and care for them,
Whenever they are near.

Lourdes Webb (11)
Shernold School, Maidstone

Rainforest

In the rainforest I am free
Nobody can control me
Creepy-crawlies running everywhere
You won't really even care.

The lovely flowers growing wildly
Tigers don't act kindly
Trees swaying in the breeze,
The water is nice and clean.

Rain is falling very heavily
The wonderful feeling is very heavenly
Different animals, surrounding lakes,
In the rainforest you could get *aches!*

Foluso Shoneyin (10)
Shernold School, Maidstone

I Know A Dog That . . .

I know a dog that . . .
has the most peculiar name
and makes a noise of an aeroplane
he doesn't bark he likes to screech
and hates playing on the beach.

I know a dog that . . .
enjoys chasing his tail
and likes to go walking up and down dale
he hates the town cats but likes all the dogs
he hops round the pond as if he's a frog.

I know a dog that . . .
has white curly hair
and likes to go on the rides at the fair
he has a best friend, his name is Borris
and the dog that I know, he's called Maurice.

Elizabeth Blenkinsop (8)
Shernold School, Maidstone

Football Match

One day I got up and looked at the clock,
I was running late, and I had a date.
Then I had a bit of a shock,
I went to see my football boss.
We started the game because we won the toss,
We kicked the ball, and ran up and down the hall.
Then the whistle blew at the end
Then I said goodbye to my friends.

Jordan Tompsett (8)
Shernold School, Maidstone

Where's Spot?

Where's Spot? He's not under the bed,
He's not in the park
Or on top of my head!

Where's Spot? He's not down the road,
He's not playing drums
On an African toad!

Where's Spot? He's not running around,
He's not doing headstands
Or making a sound!

Where's Spot? There he is,
Walking on his knees,
And chasing bumblebees.

Lauren Lethbridge (8)
Shernold School, Maidstone

Pets

When I take Titch to the park
He likes to run around and bark.

Ben liked to carry a ball
But dropped it down the vent in the hall.

Co-co the gerbil is really fat
Even fatter than a rat!

Sparky the gerbil is fun
And likes to run and play in the sun.

Chloe Funnell (8)
Shernold School, Maidstone

Summer Holidays

It's my last day of school, I cannot wait,
Maybe going snowboarding or even rollerskating!
Playing with my dog in the park,
But I'm not allowed to go after dark.
Or climbing trees so very high
I wouldn't like to jump off them and try to fly!

I'll go and visit my aunt in Smarden
We'll have water fights in her garden
Splashing water everywhere in the paddling pool
The temperatures will be very cool
At the seaside making sandcastles with my bucket and spade
We'll buy some ice cream and I'll pay!

Seaweed beneath my feet
The rockpool provides my seat
Time to go home I'm really glad
I hope I wasn't all that bad.

I wake up, what's been going on?
I thought I was at the seaside
Oh, I know what's wrong, as I sighed
I've been daydreaming!

Megan Leach (9)
Shernold School, Maidstone

Puppies

Puppies, puppies, lovely and cute,
They are naughty because they chew my best boots.
They play with me all day and roll about
They really don't like it when I shout.
I enjoy it when I take them for a walk
Their best treat is a piece of pork.

Thomas Scoley (7)
Shernold School, Maidstone

Googly Goggles

Goggles are googly and used as a gadget
Some bright colours,
Some plain,
And this is what they really do.

Goggles are a tiny bit like sunglasses
But they cover your eyes
They are transparent, so you can see through them
And stop water going inside your eyes
And then you can dive
Under the water
And swim.

Chanel Levy (9)
Shernold School, Maidstone

My Tortoise

I have a tortoise
his name is Fred,
I have a tortoise
he made his own bed.
My tortoise is cautious
when he walks round on grass,
he eats dandelions and daisies
but he is not very fast.
A lot of the time my tortoise gets stuck
in the bonfire and the bushes.
If he gets out he's full of luck.

Eleanor Pile (8)
Shernold School, Maidstone

The Lost Boy

I'm lost, I'm lost,
I don't know where to go
I'm lost, I don't know where
to go!

I hope I'm found
Instead of sitting here on
the dirty ground,
I wish I am, I wish I am found.

At last I'm found
sitting here on the dirty ground,
my wish came true, my wish came true,
I'm glad I was found
because I'm here with you!

Emily Witney (9)
Shernold School, Maidstone

Mole

There was a mole
Which was underground
Looking for a home
He looked up and down
And left and right
Then he decided to look above ground
Was it a good idea?

No!

Niroshan Ravishankar (9)
Shernold School, Maidstone

Winter

I look out of the window
I see the snow
Tumbling down
I really want to go outside
In the cold air
To build a snowman
I see the bench full of snow
I wish the snow went on
Forever
I see my mum out there
Getting the washing in
My mum with her scarf
In the cold air
Full of cold, she must be freezing.

Emily Martin (8)
Temple Ewell CE Primary School, Dover

The Tiger

Golden
Fierce
Hairy
Suspicious
Terrifying
Scary
Terminator
Sharp teeth
Mad
Fast
Stripy
Vicious.

Kenny Jones (9)
Temple Ewell CE Primary School, Dover

Highwayman

Highwayman
   Highwayman
      Ride on till dawn
         Have your sword drawn.

Highwayman
   Highwayman
      Gallop on fast
         Don't let the carriage ride on past.

Highwayman
   Highwayman
      Ride on through gusty trees
         Past stormy seas.

Highwayman
   Highwayman
      Hear the cobbles clatter
         Like glass as it shatters.

Highwayman
   Highwayman
      See the carriage ride
         Over the cobbles as it glides.

Highwayman
   Highwayman
      Cry, 'Stand and deliver!'
Highwayman
   Highwayman
      Steal all goods.

Elizabeth Williams (9)
Temple Ewell CE Primary School, Dover

Farm Visit

When I woke up in the morning
I could not believe it
It was the day that made my life
It was the farm visit.
I got dressed, brushed my teeth,
Washed my face and got my breakfast.
Then I went to the coach
It was a long visit there.
When I got there it was cool
Because we stepped in mud.
Then it started to get scary,
Other schools came
That was scary they were not nice
Because a girl from another school
Moaned at me and Katerina
But I was alright after a while.
We went back, it took about 45 minutes.
We had to wait for our parents to collect us.

Ashley Mills (8)
Temple Ewell CE Primary School, Dover

I See A Bird

I see a bird, I see a bird
Smiling at me, smiling at me.
In a tree, in a tree and I see a blackbird
I see a blackbird smiling at me, smiling at me.
Wonder what he is thinking?
I hope he is not going to eat a worm
We need worms for Earth.

Holly Gillard (8)
Temple Ewell CE Primary School, Dover

Puppies

Balls of white fur
Wet black dots
Twinkling orbs
Pink tongues licking
Fluffy faces
Tiny feet crawling.

Exploring
Stalking bugs
Tugging on slippers
Eating anything we can find
Playing in the mud.

Cuddling
Soft and furry
Mummy licking us
Time for tea
Getting tired
Goodnight.

Caroline Padfield (9)
Temple Ewell CE Primary School, Dover

Old Man Limerick

There was an old man
Who lived in a mill
And every day he took his pill
It made him laugh and laugh
As he went skipping down the path
The happy old man from the mill.

Lauren Beaney (8)
Temple Ewell CE Primary School, Dover

I Just Can't Think

Well here it goes
I cannot think
But I can blink
And I can drink
But I cannot think
Of a poem
I am just
Writing words
From my mind.
It's a medium day
Oh okay, I'm a bit bored
And that is the truth,
Other people around me
Are just thinking
Of a poem and
I'm just writing
Out of mind.

I just can't think.

Elliot Cox (8)
Temple Ewell CE Primary School, Dover

I Fell Out Of Bed

Oh no,
I fell out of bed
It felt like a sumo did a belly flop on me
Then it got off but a hotel fell on me
All the people jumped out and one had a broken leg,
An old man's walking stick had broken
And my grandad's eye fell in the pile.
I woke up and found that I was on the floor.

Finlay McMunn (8)
Temple Ewell CE Primary School, Dover

Highwayman

Riding through the woods,
Riding through the woods.
The highwayman - dark, mysterious
Riding through the woods.

A clattering carriage coming nearer,
A clattering carriage coming nearer.
Stand and deliver - your gold and girl!
A clattering carriage no more.

Escape, escape, run away,
Escape, escape run away.
How to keep this beautiful girl?
Escape, escape, run away.

Paris Bates (9)
Temple Ewell CE Primary School, Dover

There Was An Old Man From Deal

There was an old man from Deal
Who had warts on his heels
He went to the nurse
And he lost his purse
That poor old man from Deal.

Olivia Kurzawa (8)
Temple Ewell CE Primary School, Dover

Rotten Presents

I hate pants and socks,
Don't get me wrong
I wear them or else it would be drafty
But as presents they are rotten Nan.

Drew End (8)
Temple Ewell CE Primary School, Dover

Don't Climb

Don't you dare
Don't you dare climb over me
I'm a child not a tree
I have no branches these are arms
Please don't climb over me.

Georgia Berry (7)
Temple Ewell CE Primary School, Dover

There Once Was A Girl

There once was a girl called Holly
Who was put in a trolley
She was pushed down an aisle
And crashed into Finlay and Kyle.

Amber Harrison (8)
Temple Ewell CE Primary School, Dover

In The Garden

A big, slimy, slushy,
Sloppy, sloppy, sloppy,
Slow, swappy, smammy,
Fat, big snail.

Katerina Vause (7)
Temple Ewell CE Primary School, Dover

The Snowman

I would like a snowman of my own
I am so looking forward to it when it snows.
I love to go sledging
When it is your turn, don't be scared!

Kayleigh Steele (7)
Temple Ewell CE Primary School, Dover

The Highwayman

The highwayman rode
Through the misty woods
His black cape flowing
His face covered by a hood
In the distance there was a noise
Looking back the highwayman saw soldiers
Driving Sandies golden carriage
To fight for her would be the only way to win
Her heart
And save the day!
Hours passed
The battle was over
There they lay
Ten of the soldiers
Lying on the floor
The highwayman had killed them all
Out of the carriage she came
She slowly untied her hair
She walked towards him.

They walked away hand in hand . . .

Charlotte Ward (9)
Temple Ewell CE Primary School, Dover

There Was An Old Man

There was an old man
Who got stuck in a van
Nobody knew he was there
Six months went past
Very, very fast
Two inches grew his hair.

Hollie Pain (8)
Temple Ewell CE Primary School, Dover

I Remember . . .

I remember
His grin that stretched from ear to ear
I remember
His big warm jumper that was big, green and thick.
I remember
His big appetite for meat and vegetables
I remember
His bald head that was as hard as a rock
I remember
How he snorted in his sleep
I remember
When he built a tree house
And the next day it fell down!
I remember
His big glaring eyes that stared at me all the time
I remember
Him leaving his dirty socks all over the house
And me having to pick them up
I remember
How he left a sweaty patch on the back of the sofa
after a day at work.

I miss him.

Rachel Grant (9)
Temple Ewell CE Primary School, Dover

Last Night

Last night my tele went off automatically
It was 2.00 in the morning.
There were shadows dancing on the wall,
The landing was spinning around
And I couldn't see
And then I heard my tele.
That was last night.

Jason Mallory (8)
Temple Ewell CE Primary School, Dover

Not Now Kenny

Not now Kenny
I am really busy
I need to go to work
So don't be with Lizzy.

Not now Kenny
I need to practice dance
I am going to a disco
So you have a chance.

Not now Kenny
Don't be a jerk
I need to go to lunch
And next time don't perk.

Not now Kenny
I am going for a swim
So call a taxi to Nan
And act slim.

Not now Kenny
I need to fix the car
So be good
And fill the jar.

Not now Kenny
Time for dinner
Put your napkin on
And first one to eat their dinner
Is the winner!

Callum Moorin (9)
Temple Ewell CE Primary School, Dover

Anxious Alex

Anxious Alex went to a palace
When Alex saw the palace
We were a bit malice, then anxious Alex
Went back to his normal palace.

Ashley Tse (8)
Temple Ewell CE Primary School, Dover

The Werewolf

He lives in a hole
Underground
He howls
In the morning

He has sharp teeth
That bite proudly
He goes out at night
And sniffs out prey

He bites his prey
And puts in poison
He rips and tears
Chews all the meat

Once he has eaten all the meat
He takes the bones back to his young . . .

Matthew Bryant (8)
Temple Ewell CE Primary School, Dover

A Poem About Unicorns

White, fluffy coat with a silver mane shines a light on the trees
A horn that sparkles with bronze and silver weaved around it
Gold, silky, delicate wings make them fly in the sky
And glitter falling down from the
Trail they leave behind them
If you ever see the trail
Make a wish
And one day
You may
Become a
Unicorn.

Katie Williams (9)
Temple Ewell CE Primary School, Dover

The Dragon

Eyes
Red and inferno
Glistening
In the light

Claws
Sharp and slashy
Shining
Terrifying

Wings
Large and monstrous
Panting
Beating

Teeth
Jagged and dagger-like
Tearing
Ripping.

Dominic Hayles (9)
Temple Ewell CE Primary School, Dover

Stars

As I sit on my bed
                As I stare out of my window
Watching the
        Sparkling stars
                glowing in
the misty sky
        the darkness of one night
is lit up by the
        golden stars
            glistening.

Carla Reid (8)
Temple Ewell CE Primary School, Dover

Dolphins

A wet nose
       upon my face
              it's soft and silky.
Splish sposh goes
      the animal that
            has blue, twinkling
eyes that shine like diamonds,
crystals that shimmer in the
night.
It's voice is like a soft
      tune talking to all the other
      dolphins silently, they get softer
           and softer
they talk lovingly and quietly.

Chloe Thomson (9)
Temple Ewell CE Primary School, Dover

The Dragon

Eyes
    Big and bright
Ears
    Pointy and hearing
Tongue
    Red and watery
Nose
    Long and freckly
Teeth
    Huge and blunt.
Face
    Old and friendly.

Luke Hind (9)
Temple Ewell CE Primary School, Dover

Tuna

Grey
　Flaky
　　Shiny
　Wet
　　Heavy
　　　Soft
　　　　Squishy
　　　　　Squashy
　　　　Vinegary
　　　　　Watery
　　　　Tasty
　　　Runny
　　　　Gooey
　　　　Sticky
　　　Slushy
　　　　Chewy
　　　　　Crunchy
　　　　Munchy.
Mouth-watering.

Becky Matthews (8)
Temple Ewell CE Primary School, Dover

Stars

Look up here
The stars look like nocturnal torches
In the misty twilight sky
Like the blazing essence of light.

In the freedom of descending darkness.

George Smissen (9)
Temple Ewell CE Primary School, Dover

Spaghetti

Lacy shoes
Wiggly worms
Look like big fat worms

Slimy wiggly
Wiggle in my hands
Slithers through my hands

It feels all saucy
Tomato
Beans and tomato

I chop it up
Like a cheese grater
It goes to the back of my throat
And slithers down . . .

Jessica Dowle (9)
Temple Ewell CE Primary School, Dover

I Am A Snowman

I am a snowman
As cold as can be
I glisten like the stars in the ruby rings

I am a snowman
As happy as can be
Watching the children
Play happily

I am a snowman
As sad as can be
The children are gone
And I am fading slightly.

Cerys Wilmshurst (8)
Temple Ewell CE Primary School, Dover

Stars

Look up in the sky
At the twinkling silver stars
Like sequins
They shine and shimmer
Dancing in the night sky
Like sparklers on firework night
Magically sending out the light

Stars . . .

James Phillips (8)
Temple Ewell CE Primary School, Dover

If I Was A Teacher . . .

If I was a teacher
I would make school fun,
I'd do the same sum every day,
'What is one add one?'

If I was a teacher
Class would never be a snooze
It would be like a holiday
Or even like a cruise.

If I was a teacher
My class would never be quiet
And everyday I was there
I would tell them to start a riot.

If I was a teacher
I would teach until nine
But then I would go out and tell everyone,
'Go on out, it's home time!'

If I was a teacher
I wouldn't be mean or cruel,
I would make my pupils happy
So they'll *want* to come to school!

Sadie Smurthwaite (10)
Upton Primary School, Bexleyheath

Little Dog

There is a little dog
Who sits amongst the birds
Sitting there, sitting there, all day long.
Never, never, moving
Never, never, scratching
Sitting there, sitting there, all day long.

The same little dog
Who sat amongst the birds
Waited and waited for the sunset to come
Never, never, stirring
Never, never, barking
Waiting and waiting for the sunset to come.

Emily Giles (8)
Upton Primary School, Bexleyheath

My Wedding

My wedding, my wedding, where is the groom?
The groom is at home fixing his perfume.
My wedding, my wedding, where is the priest?
The priest is outside playing catch the old beast.
My wedding, my wedding, where are the mums?
The mums are at home cleaning their sons,
Oh dear, oh dear, did things go right?
The wedding is over now please say goodnight.
No, oh no 'cause this is a day!
That we celebrate and you pray.
Call the groom and the mums and their sons,
Tell them that the wedding's still on.

Colina Archie-Pearce (9)
Upton Primary School, Bexleyheath

The Little Cat

The little cat
Was sitting and sitting
And waiting and waiting
Till the cat food came in.

The little cat
Had a rat beside her
That sat on the mat
With a disappointing feel.

The little cat
Was not really good at playing ball at all
But at least the cat had a good midnight feast.

The little cat
Had a fright in the night
When the rat came in again
With a good feeling this time.

Lucy Robinson (9)
Upton Primary School, Bexleyheath

Summer

S unny summer coming our way, we're waiting for the summer days!
U nderneath the apple tree, if you bend down carefully,
   pick up an apple for you and me!
M ake your summer special, make your summer long,
   make your summer song, all day long!
M ates, family, young ones too, bring them to your summer,
   just make sure you're there too!
E ating favourite lollies, sugarplum too, eat all these yummies
   coz they're for you too!
R espect all these toys and sweets, coz on the other side
   of the world there are no treats!

Zara Nosratpour (9)
Upton Primary School, Bexleyheath